BLESSING:

ANNIHILATOR OF SORROW

DAVID S. PHILEMON

Royal Diadem Publishing INC

Book Title: BLESSING: Annihilator Of Sorrow
Author: DAVID S. PHILEMON
Phone Number: +1773 521 3954
Email Address: info.royaldiadempublishing@gmail.com

This book was designed and published by:

Royal Diadem Publishing INC
☐ info.royaldiadempublishing@gmail.com
☐+1773 521 3954

All scripture quoted are taken from King James Version of the Bible

Dedication

May this book, BLESSING: Annihilator of Sorrow, be a doorway to hope, a wellspring of joy, and a guide to divine abundance. With every page, may sorrow be replaced by peace, doubt be replaced by faith, and every reader discover the overflowing blessings that await. Let this work awaken hearts, inspire transformation, and release the fullness of life that was always meant to be theirs.

ACKNOWLEDGEMENT

This book would not have been possible without the unwavering support, dedication, and talent of an extraordinary team. My deepest gratitude goes to each of you for your contributions, insights, and encouragement throughout this journey.

First and foremost, thank you to Rev. Mimi Philemon, my dear wife; my brother-in-law, Rev. Shina Gentry; my Assistant Pastor, Rev. Bright Amudoaghan; and the Lead Pastor of Church on Fire International, Pastor Peculiar Onyekere, for your incredible effort, encouragement, and steadfast belief in this project. Your support has been instrumental in bringing this vision to life.

To the dedicated leaders of Royal Diadem Publishing, Ide Imogie and Kishawna Bailey, I am immensely grateful for believing in this project from the very beginning and for investing your time and energy into its development. Your creativity, dedication, and expertise have been the backbone of this endeavor.
I am especially thankful to the entire Royal Diadem Publishing team for your meticulous attention to detail, refining every page, and ensuring that each word reflects our shared vision.

A heartfelt thank you to my family, friends, and colleagues, whose unwavering encouragement and faith in this work gave me the courage and strength to see it through.

Finally, to all the readers and supporters who give meaning to these pages thank you. I am humbled and honored to share this journey with each of you.

With all my gratitude, David Philemon

Special Call To Salvation & New Beginnings From Apostle Dr. David Philemon

Dear Beloved, You are not reading this by accident God Himself has led you here because He loves you more than you could ever imagine. No matter where you've been, what you've done, or how far you feel from Him, His arms are open wide to receive you today.

The Bible says in John 3:16: *"For God so loved the world that He gave His one and only Son, that whoever believes in Him shall not perish but have eternal life."* That means you. Jesus Christ came to take away your sins, heal your heart, and give you a brand-new life one filled with peace, purpose, and hope.

Today, you can step into that new life. If you are ready to surrender to Him, pray this from your heart:
The Salvation Prayer Heavenly Father, I come to You in the name of Jesus. I confess that I am a sinner in need of Your mercy. I believe that Jesus Christ is Your Son, that He died on the cross for my sins, and that You raised Him from the dead. Today, I turn away from my old life and give You my whole heart. Jesus, come into my life. Be my Lord, my Savior, and my best friend. Wash me clean, fill me with Your Holy Spirit, and guide me into the life You created me to live. Thank You, Father, for loving me, forgiving me, and making me Yours. In Jesus' name, Amen.
Welcome to the Family of God! If you prayed that prayer with faith, congratulations! Your sins are forgiven, your name is written in the Book of Life, and heaven is celebrating you right now. This is the beginning of the greatest journey you will ever take and you are not alone.

Your Next Steps:

* Connect with a Bible-believing church: You were never meant to walk this journey alone.
* Read God's Word daily: The Bible will show you who God is and who you are in Him.
* Pray often: Talk to God about everything. He delights in hearing your voice.
* Share your testimony: Let others know what God has done for you.

Your life will never be the same again. God's plans for you are greater than you can imagine so walk forward in faith, knowing He is with you every step of the way.

CONTENTS

INTRODUCTION

God said to Abraham, "I will bless you, and I will make you a blessing." For over 24 years, Abraham walked that promise into his life, achieving material, physical, and financial substance. He attained great heights and became a respected and feared name in society because God said, "I will." God kept His word, and one day He showed up again and said, "Hey, remember I told you I was going to bless you?"
But Abraham replied,

> "Lord, do not just talk to me about material things. There are certain things more important than having cars and houses and all these material possessions."

Abraham looked at his life and said, "I have all these things, but who will be the benefactor? Who's going to enjoy this?" He thought, "I will let my servant Eliezer, born in my house, be my heir."

In Genesis 15, I want you to see something in verse one. Remember, God said to him in Genesis 12, "I will bless you; I will make your name great." By Genesis 13, verse 2, Abraham had become rich in silver, gold, and cattle. How did God make his name great? God allowed certain people to cross his path negatively. In Africa, we say, "show them pepper." So, God showed his enemy's pepper!

They were not really his enemies, but somehow God dealt with those who took something from him, and they started paying him back. How did Abraham become rich? Among other things, he was compensated. When he went down to Egypt, and Pharaoh paid him lots of money, silver and gold. Even in his mistakes, God honored His promise: *"I will bless you."* During the famine, he went down to Egypt (Genesis 12), and after that, God said, *"Abraham, you need to come out of Egypt."*

So, Abraham came out, but this time in Genesis 13:2, he left with silver, gold, and cattle. Why? Abraham went up out of Egypt with his wife and all he had, along with Lot. Abraham was very rich in cattle, silver, and gold. In verse 3, he journeyed from the south to Bethel, to the place where his tent had been at the beginning, between Bethel and Ai, and there he raised an altar.

Verse 5 tells us that Lot, who went with Abraham, had flocks, herds, and tents. Wow! You see, the blessing that came upon Abraham rubbed off on Lot. How did they get all this? The Bible says it was because Pharaoh, the king of Egypt, had paid Abraham for Sarah, his wife. Now, just to clarify, he did not sleep with her; Abraham did not pimp his wife. Pharaoh saw her beauty, and God made him pay. So, get ready! God is about to use what men think is impossible to bless you! God want to use this book to break every strong force that keeps you many years in sorrow.

CHAPTER ONE

THE CONSEQUENCES
OF PLANTING
BITTER SEEDS

Most people spend their time asking God for a brilliant future while their present and past are corrupted and so messed up. If the seed you are holding in your hand to plant for your future is a bitter seed, there is no way that bitter seed can produce sweet fruit. The seed will always produce after its kind. Sometimes you have good seeds, and it is easier for those good seeds to be corrupted and produce bad fruit than for bad seeds to produce good fruit. Do you understand? It is easier for good parents raising good children to face challenges that might spoil their kids than for bad parents trying to raise good children.

Since the fall of man, life has become so weak that whenever evil shows up, it often seems stronger than good. Whether you like it or not, God said to Adam, *"If you eat this fruit, in dying you shall die."* The king James version tells us that the day you eat it, you shall surely die. But the original Hebrew says, *"In dying, thou shalt die,"* meaning you will activate death for the entire human race. From that moment, everything you touch will begin to die.

Death leads downward. That is why when you hear *"hell,"* you think of something downwards. It is always easier to slide down than to climb up. When was the last time you slid down and had to catch your breath? You do not try to catch your breath when sliding down; in fact, you have fun! If you are driving, you can take your foot off the accelerator. You have to make sure your foot is on the brake when you are sliding. But try that when climbing a hill! You will not just be stagnant; if you are not careful, even your car, if it is not in good shape, can start going in the wrong direction.

So, when you talk about life in the natural, God has already sentenced anyone outside the garden to eat from the sweat of their face. He said,

> *"You will eat bread from the sweat of your face" (Genesis 3:19).*

The verdict is clear; the sentence is clear. That is why, when Jesus came, after His death, the first thing He did was descend. He went down to handle the matters below. And when He rose again, the Bible says He ascended, and the disciples watched Him. He was blessing them.

That is why the best thing that can happen to anyone is to be in Christ. Christianity is not a religion; it is a relationship with Christ. Every time people leave their lives to chance, I promise you, no matter how lucky things may seem. Chance will always overtake luck because chance works with the wind. That is why some people build things, and They do not last because their lives are governed by chance, those things can easily get wiped out. The moment a person starts raising, they begin insuring everything. Why? Because they are afraid of losing them.

But the blessing of God is different. When it comes upon a person, it becomes a force that fights against decay and decline. The blessing of God becomes like an elevator, lifting you to heights beyond your imagination. That is why you must fight for the blessing. Do not just sit and say, *"If He wants to bless me, He will bless me."* That is the spirit of Esau, making a spiritual son or daughter neglect the need for the authentic blessing of the father.

The blessing is so valuable that God commanded the priests. He told Moses,

> *"This is how you shall bless the people, for I want to put My name on them, but I cannot do it illegally" (Numbers 6:27).*

No matter how good you are, you cannot bless yourself to the point of being okay. *"For without contradiction, the lesser is blessed by the greater."* So, no matter who you are or where you are, you can never rise higher than the one who blesses you.

When someone is blessing you, God says it should be done in the name of those who have already obtained the blessing. So, when someone is authorized to bless and begins to speak over your life, just as I am blessing you now, I am not giving you from my personal encounters with God, I am giving you from my legitimate spiritual lineage; men and women who have walked with God and have proven records that have also impact me.

Not everyone that comes out of nowhere can just start pronouncing blesses upon you. You need to know how far will that blessing take you, how high can it lift you. You cannot just say, *"I bless myself."* It is good to speak blessings over yourself, do not get me wrong, always bless yourself but when it comes to truly winning in life, you must be blessed by someone authorized to do so.

Look at Hannah. She prayed for years and years. But one day while praying Eli added his prayer to hers, at once, the case was resolved, issue solved. That is the difference. Just one word can turn things around.

Restoration Amidst Mistakes

Even Abraham was paid for his mistake, who gets paid for their mistakes? I will tell you; it is only the blessed one. If the blessing is upon your life, you get paid for making a mistake. But you are going to see what kind of blessing gets you paid, lest you go back now and start looking for mistakes to make. Then you will end up spending 25 years fixing one hour of foolishness. That is said.

Abraham suddenly became rich. Every material thing imaginable was given to Abraham.

> Genesis 15:1, 3 (LBT) said: "Afterward, Jehovah spoke to Abraham in a vision, and this is what He told him: Do not be fearful, God is happy—hey, my friend Abraham—for I will defend you, and I will give you a great blessin.... But Abraham replied, O Lord Jehovah, what good are all Your blessings when I have no son?"

Now, just two chapters ago, Abraham was doing just fine. He had employees, he had possessions, he had everything a man could want. Then suddenly, he realized that as good as material things are, they still do not satisfy the deepest longings of the heart.

This is why Jesus said in Matthew 6:33,

> "But seek ye first the kingdom of God, and his righteousness; and all these things shall be added unto you."

You see, Jesus understood something fundamental about the nature of material possessions. Everything material, no matter how precious or valuable it might seem, is subject to four inescapable fates. And we need to understand these fates if we are going to live a life that is truly blessed and not just materially comfortable.

They Can Be Stolen

Everything material that you possess can be stolen. It does not matter if it is locked up in a bank vault or hidden under your mattress, if it is physical, it can be taken from you. This is not just my opinion; it is a truth that Jesus Himself emphasized. In Matthew 6:19-20, He says,

> "Lay not up for yourselves treasures upon earth, where moth and rust doth corrupt, and where thieves break through and steal: But lay up for yourselves treasures in heaven, where neither moth nor rust doth corrupt, and where thieves do not break through nor steal."

You see, Jesus is pointing out the vulnerability of earthly possessions. No matter how secure you think your stuff is, there is always a risk of theft. Think about it, how many people do you know who have had their homes broken into, their cars stolen, or their identities compromised? It happens all the time, and it can happen to anyone, regardless of how wealthy or careful they are.

But here is the thing when you are walking in God is blessing, even if something is stolen from you, it does not have the power to destroy you. Why? Because your true wealth, your true value, is not in those material possessions. It is in your relationship with God and the divine favor that rests upon your life.

Job had everything, wealth, health, family - and in one day, it was all taken from him. Thieves came and stole his livestock; his wealth was wiped out to give sorrow to job. But what did Job say? In Job 1:21, he declared,

> "Naked came I out of my mother's womb, and naked shall

I return thither: the LORD gave, and the LORD hath taken away; blessed be the name of the LORD."

Even in the face of such devastating loss, Job understood that his true wealth was not in his possessions, but in his relationship with God.

So, when we talk about things being stolen, we are not just talking about physical theft. We are talking about anything that can be taken from you against your will. It could be your reputation through slander, your time through unnecessary obligations, or your peace of mind through worry and anxiety. All of these are forms of theft that the enemy uses to try and rob you of your blessing.

They Can Rust

The second fate that befalls material things they can rust. When I say rust, I am not just talking about metal oxidizing, though that is certainly part of it. I am talking about the gradual deterioration that happens to everything in this physical world. Nothing material lasts forever, everything is subject to wear and tear, to breaking down over time.

This principle is so important that it is mentioned multiple times. Jesus says,

"Lay not up for yourselves treasures upon earth, where moth and rust doth corrupt, and where thieves break through and steal. Matthew 6:19 "

He is pointing out that even if our possessions are not stolen, they are still subject to natural decay.

Think about it, how many things have you owned that have worn out over time? Clothes that fade and tear, cars that break down, electronics that become obsolete. Even our own bodies, which are in a sense our most valuable material possession, are subject to aging and decay. As it says in Ecclesiastes 12:7,

"Then shall the dust return to the earth as it was: and the spirit shall return unto God who gave it."

The beautiful thing about walking in God is blessing even as our outer man is decaying, our inner man is being renewed day by day. The Apostle Paul puts it this way in 2 Corinthians 4:16:

"For which cause we faint not; but though our outward man perish, yet the inward man is renewed day by day."

You see, when you are blessed by God, you have access to a kind of wealth that does not rust. It is a spiritual wealth, a richness of soul that grows stronger and more vibrant with each passing day. This is why it is so important to invest in your spiritual life, to cultivate your relationship with God. Because while everything else in this world is rusting away, your spirit can be growing, expanding, becoming more and more like Christ.

And here is another thing, when you are walking in God is blessing, even the things that do rust can be miraculously preserved or restored. Think about the children of Israel in the wilderness. The Bible tells us in Deuteronomy 29:5,

"And I have led you forty years in the wilderness: your clothes are not waxen old upon you, and thy shoe is not waxen old upon thy foot."

For forty years, their clothes and shoes did not wear out! That is the kind of supernatural preservation that comes with God is blessing.

They Can Decay

While rusting is about gradual wear and tear, decay is about the breaking down of the very substance of a thing. It is about things rotting, decomposing, falling apart at their very core. This principle of decay is deeply embedded in the fabric of our physical universe. Scientists call it entropy, the tendency of all systems to move from order to disorder over time. But long before scientists discovered this law, the Bible was already teaching us about the reality of decay.

In Romans 8:21, Paul writes,

"Because the creature itself also shall be delivered from the bondage of corruption into the glorious liberty of the children of God."

The word *"corruption"* here refers to decay, to the breaking down of creation itself. Paul is saying that the entire created order is subject to this law of decay.

Think about food left out too long, or a house left unmaintained, or even a business that is not properly managed. All of these things, if left to themselves, will decay. There will break down, fall apart, cease to function as they were intended to.

But here is where the blessing of God comes in. When you are walking in God is favor, you have access to a power that can arrest decay, that can bring life out of death, that can restore what seems beyond repair.

Look at the story of Lazarus in John 11. By the time Jesus arrived, Lazarus had been dead for four days. His body would have been in an advanced state of decay. But Jesus, the source of all life, spoke one word *"Lazarus, come forth"* and decay was reversed, death was defeated, and Lazarus walked out of that tomb alive!

That is the power available to you when you are blessed by God. Even when things in your life seem to be decaying your dreams, your relationships, your health God can speak a word and bring restoration. As it says in Joel 2:25,

> *"And I will restore to you the years that the locust hath eaten, the cankerworm, and the caterpiller, and the palmerworm, my great army which I sent among you."*

You see, in God is economy, nothing is ever truly lost. What looks like decay to us can be the setup for a miraculous restoration in God is hands.

They Can Lose Value

This is perhaps the most insidious of all, because it can happen even when an object remains physically intact. Something can be in perfect condition, free from rust or decay, and yet still become worthless overnight. Think about it, how many things have you owned that were once valuable but are now practically worthless? Maybe it is a piece of technology that is become obsolete, or a fashion item that is gone out of style, or an investment that is taken. The truth is, in this world, value is often fleeting and unpredictable.

In Proverbs 23:5, it says,

> *"Wilt thou set thine eyes upon that which is not? for riches certainly make themselves wings; they fly away as an eagle toward heaven."*

The writer is warning us about the transient nature of wealth, how quickly it can lose its value and slip away from us.

But here is the amazing thing about walking in God is blessing your true value is not determined by the things you possess or by the opinions of others. Your value comes from your identity as a child of God, and that value never diminishes. As it says in 1 Peter 2:9,

"But ye are a chosen generation, a royal priesthood, an holy nation, a peculiar people; that ye should shew forth the praises of him who hath called you out of darkness into his marvellous light."

When you are blessed by God, you have a worth that transcends market fluctuations or cultural trends. You are valuable not because of what you own or whatyou have achieved, but because of whose you are. And that value can never be taken away from you. Moreover, when you are walking in God is blessing, even the things in your life that seem to have lost their value can be redeemed and repurposed. God has a way of taking what the world considers worthless and making it priceless. Just look at the cross, an instrument of torture and shame that God transformed into the symbol of our salvation.

So do not get too caught up in the changing values of this world. Instead, invest in the things that have eternal value, your relationship with God, your character, your love for others. As Jesus said in Matthew 6:20,

"But lay up for yourselves treasures in heaven, where neither moth nor rust doth corrupt, and where thieves do not break through nor steal."

So, imagine a person who spends all his life trying to get rich, spreading everything in his life just trying to gather material things. You want to build your dream home, but before you finish building it, it has expired because everything is changing. It is funny how people are going back to mobile homes now. Is not that crazy?

But we are still going to build castles, live in castles. Yeah, we can have 32,000 mobile homes in our castle, but we are going to have our castle. But, if all that controls your life are these things that decay in value, your life will be miserable. That is why God wants to give you the blessing, the power that stabilizes your life and puts you on a pedestal that never sinks. And when the blessing is on you, it arrests sorrow.

What Is Sorrow?

Anything that brings you to a place of loss, anything that brings you to a place where you rust, anything that brings you to a place where you decay, and anything that brings you to a place where you lose value. Abraham said, for what use is all this money if I have no son? I am going without a son to carry my legacy. Without a son, some other member of my family household will inherit all my wealth.

You can have children, but if they are children of sorrow, it is as good as not having any. Children who cannot think, children who cannot make sense of their lives, children who will not press in to fight for their own destiny, it is as good as not having anything. I pray for you that the blessing of God will eliminate uselessness in the lives of your children.

Sometimes how God handles this kind of thing is to give you so many that the ones who are useless will be so insignificant that the useful ones will overshadow the useless ones. God told me,

> *"Son, I want you to keep focusing on Me and raise with all your heart your sons and daughters and the people I bring to you. I will make sure that your useful and significant sons and daughters will be so outstanding that their glory will invalidate the useless ones."*

You will be so successful that if a member of the church decides not to be successful, your success will shine so brightly that nobody will even know those ones exist because they can come into your glory. And it will look it, it is their glory, and you will not care because you have enough glory.

The Power Of Intentional Prayer

Nothing, and I mean absolutely nothing, makes your life amazing like intelligent prayer. You know, people often wonder why Jabez's prayer worked so powerfully. Well, let me break it down for you it was an intentional, intelligently calculated prayer. He did not just throw out some vague wishes or mumble some half-hearted requests. No, Jabez knew exactly what he wanted and he was not afraid to ask for it.

Look at what he prayed in 1 Chronicles 4:10,

> "And Jabez called on the God of Israel, saying, Oh that thou wouldest bless me indeed, and enlarge my coast, and that thine hand might be with me, and that thou wouldest keep me from evil, that it may not grieve me! And God granted him that which he requested".

Jabez gave God five to seven things straight up, no beating around the bush, and guess what? God gave him everything he asked for. That is the power of intentional prayer, friends. It is about being specific, being bold, and being intentional with your requests.

Now, I want to speak something powerful over your lives. I decree, and I mean this with every fiber of my being, that you will become so significant, your glory will be so radiant and so unmistakable, that even people without any glory of their own, when they hang around you, your glory will be the glory they brag on and hide under. That is how bright you are going to shine, in the mighty name of Jesus. But here is the kicker you will not need to hide under anybody else's glory because you will be a star in your own

DAVID S. PHILEMON

right, a shining light so bright you will be like a sun of your own.

So, Abraham said, *"Another family member will inherit my wealth."* Can you feel the disappointment, the unfulfillment in those words? But then, oh boy, listen to what God told him. The Lord said, *"No, no one else will be your heir, for you will have a son to inherit everything you own."*

This is not just about having biological children. Do not get me wrong, biological children are a blessing, but I am talking about something bigger here. I am talking about having significant, influential children's spiritual sons and daughters whose lives are a pure reflection of honor, beauty, glory, and stature. I am talking about leaving a legacy that goes beyond just passing on material wealth.

when the blessing of God sits on a man, it does not just stop there. It rests upon you too, and it flows through you to others. You will be able to release strength and favor to those around you. You are not just going to scrape by in life, barely making ends meet. No, you are going to have your own business, your own company, your own home, your own success, your own job. You will have your health, and above all, you will have all that God has planned for you. That is the kind of abundance I am talking about!

Now, let's look at what God did next with Abraham. In Genesis 15:5, the Living Bible Translation puts it this way:

> *"And God brought Abraham outside beneath the nighttime sky and told him, 'Look up into the heavens and count the stars, if you can. Your descendants will be like that—too many to count.'"*

Can you imagine that moment? Abraham, standing under the vast expanse of the night sky, trying to count stars that seemed to go on forever. That is the kind of abundance God had in mind for him, and that is the kind of abundance God has in mind for you too.

14

You see, Abraham got to a place where, at first, he thought having silver, gold, and cattle was a testimony. He thought he had it made with all his material possessions. But then he soon realized the futility of material accumulation. He understood that there is nothing material that you have that is truly satisfying in the deepest sense. Now, do not get me wrong. It is good to have means of mobility, to have resources at your disposal. But do not think for a second that when you become a millionaire, your life is automatically settled. In fact, let me tell you something when you become a millionaire, you have a million problems. That is the truth, plain and simple.

Remember what God said to Abraham back in Genesis 12:2? He said, "*I will bless you and make you a blessing.*" That is a powerful promise, but it is also a responsibility. God does not just bless us for our own benefit. He blesses us so that we can be a blessing to others. You have come to a place now where you are starting to realize that all this money, all these things you are trying so hard to acquire, in the end, they make no sense if they are not connected to something bigger than yourself. It has to be wrapped around a greater purpose. You have to understand that we are entering into a phase where your life will become the prayer point of others. The angels of God are working things out in ways you cannot even imagine.

If you let the blessing rest upon you, if you open yourself up to the fullness of what God wants to do in your life, amazing things will happen. Remember what God said to Abraham? "*You are asking Me for a son? I will not give you just a son; I will give you stars that you will not be able to count.*" That is in Genesis 15:5. God did not just meet Abraham's request, He exceeded it beyond anything Abraham could have imagined.

And yet, here is the beautiful thing, each of these "*stars*", these descendants of Abraham, they have their own level of glory. The Bible says in 1 Corinthians 15:41,

"*One star differeth from another star in glory.*"

Every star of Abraham, every descendant, every person touched by this blessing, gets to decide the level of glory they walk in. But the one thing Abraham was assured of was that every seed that comes from him will be a star.

Now, God did mention that there would be some that would be like sand not trusted, not shining. But then there are those that will be stars. And among those stars, *"One star differs from another star in glory."* That is the beauty of it - we each have our own unique glory to shine.

So, I want to pray for you. I pray, with all the authority given to me, that whenever people talk about the difference in the glory of stars, your own star will be the most enviable one. In the name of Jesus, your light will shine so bright that it will catch the attention of heaven and earth. Amen.

You see, this is what intentional prayer can do. It can take you from a place of lack, a place of unfulfillment, to a place of abundance and purpose. It can transform not just your life, but the lives of generations to come. That is the power we are tapping into when we pray with intention and intelligence.

So, do not just pray vague, general prayers. Be specific. Be bold. Be intentional. Tell God exactly what you need, exactly what you want Him to do in your life. And then, get ready. Because when you pray like that, when you approach God with that kind of faith and clarity, He does not just answer, He goes above and beyond. Remember, your prayer life is not just about getting things from God. It is about aligning yourself with His purposes, about positioning yourself to be a conduit of His blessings to others. When you pray intentionally, you are not just changing your circumstances, you are changing your destiny.

CHAPTER TWO

THE WEIGHT
OF PROPHETIC
PROMISES AND THEIR
RESPONSIBILITIES

After Abraham received that word from God, he was over the moon, happy as a clam. he went on his merry way, thinking everything was sorted. but you know what? several years down the line, that word still hadn't come to pass. and let me tell you why because no matter how "Abrahamic" you think you are, if you are not careful, you will miss what god is really saying.

God gave Abraham this incredible promise, but Abraham never took the time to ask God about the demands, the expectations. he never said, *"God, how can I make this a reality in my life?"* he just did not. and that is where many of us mess up too.

you get a prophetic word, and what do you do? you rejoice, you jump up and down like you have won the lottery, and then you go on your merry way. one year later, you are scratching your head, asking, *"where is that prophecy at?"* it is like ordering a package and never checking the tracking number. you are just sitting there, waiting for it to magically appear on your doorstep.

Abraham told his wife about the promise, and Sarah, bless her heart, she said, *"oh, I know, babe. I know how we can help God out here."* you see that girl we brought from Egypt? Abraham did not just pick-up silver and gold in Egypt. He picked up sorrow too. Folks, sorrows are constantly haunting blessings. you cannot change this. the only time it will not happen this way is after this earth is consumed and thrown into the lake of fire.

Anything and everything good attract something bad. it is like a universal law. light attracts insects. honey, sweet as it is, attracts bees. sugar attracts ants. and let's not forget, sugar causes sickness like diabetes. everything good is haunted by sorrow. that is why the blessing you walk in matters a whole lot more than you might think. I am not saying your career brings sorrow. but sorrow haunts any and everything that is good. So, your blessing, it is got to be potent enough. that is why when God showed up and was telling Abraham in genesis 15:1, the first thing he said was, *"I am your protector and your defender"* (living bible translation). because blessing has to have enough power not just power to stop sorrow from attaching itself to it, but if sorrow does manage to attach itself, it has the power to neutralize that sorrow.

my goal here (and I want you to really get this) is to ensure that the blessing of God eliminates the sorrows around your life and any sorrow that might be hunting you down. Let me tell you, it is downright foolish for you to live your life without preparing for sorrow. oh yeah, it is foolish alright. I used to tell this story about somebody that God used me to help in all manner of ways. I mean, I   poured out blessing after blessing on this person. only to find out later that it was the same person who was stealing from me. can you believe that? why would you steal from the one who has not withheld anything from you? such a thing is bad enough to cause sorrow. But you know what? I look at my heart, and I am so grateful to God that I do not have sorrow of heart.

One thing that stands, and you can take this to the bank. Nobody steals from David Philemon and lives to tell a good story. it is not possible, and i promise you, I am not bragging. the reason is simple; I have never withheld good from anyone. everything I have, I have for people. go and check how much I spend on myself. its peanuts compared to what I pour out on others. but no matter how good you are, sorrow is hunting. it is always out there, looking for a way in. but there is a thing that protects you, it eliminates sorrow. as you continue to rise in life, I decree you will not sink in sorrow, in the name of Jesus.

So, as soon as God finished giving Abraham this promise, Satan swooped in with a good alternative. Let me tell you, the alternatives of the devil, more often than not, are the magnets that pull sorrow to us. most times, these magnets may not reveal that they have captured sorrow until the sorrows start tormenting, afflicting, and messing up our lives.

The challenge was not that Hagar was Hagar. let's get that straight. the only person in that whole lineage who did not have multiple wives was Isaac. You look at Jacob, he had four women (two he married and two from his wife's maids) and before you start condemning him, let me tell you, it was legal back then. a woman who wanted to have a baby but couldn't would give her slave to her husband, and the husband would impregnate the slave. When the woman is having the baby, she would give birth in between the legs of her mistress, symbolizing that the child belonged to the mistress.

Now, you are the one to choose whether to be the baby mama of your boss's husband or to marry someone else, right? so most of these slave women, being slaves, were not married. but because they were personal slaves to the mistress, they had to cooperate. now, while no one forced anybody, when she became pregnant, it was seen as a matter of joy to have multiple children in those days. the baby would be born in between the mistress's legs. Jacob had his wife, but the servant girls which is wife's give him have more babies, and all the babies were counted by God as the 12 tribes of Israel.

So, it is not the fact that Sarah did something wrong, it was a tradition that was practiced. she actually did something that was considered right. the only reason it was wrong was because:

- she was trying to help God.
- Where they picked Hagar from. Egypt was a form of darkness, and that is where they picked Hagar from (genesis 16:1).

They were now trying to help God. they misinterpreted what God was doing, and Sarah gave in to her sorrow. because when God gives you the blessing and sorrow haunts you, you have to win over sorrow. I am not sure but if Sarah had used one of the girls that she raised herself, we would not have had this situation. but of course, she should never do, because God was working on something specific with her life. God wanted Abraham to be a reward system unto Sarah. God had spoken, and Sarah never heard her own portion. (Genesis 18:10-12).

Then Sarah made a mistake. in the very next chapter, she Gave Hagar to Abraham, and with one encounter, Hagar became pregnant and gave birth to another sorrow. this time, it was Abraham's sorrow. but the blessing of God makes rich and adds no sorrow (Proverbs 10:22).

Later, when Sarah gave birth to Isaac, the same Ishmael wanted to kill Isaac (Genesis 21:9-10). Sarah looked, and she said, *"hey honey, get rid of my sorrow. Get rid of this woman and her baby."* She said, *"this boy will not participate in this blessing."* God gave Ishmael his own blessing to settle him, but unfortunately, Sarah and Abraham had already embraced a sorrow.

whatever situation you have found yourself in, i want you to count on the integrity of God is word. because God said he will bless you, he will make your life significant, he will make your life amazing. if you have not received the material manifestation, it does not mean God is a liar, and it does not mean God has forgotten about you. Has the God of heaven forgotten any? hear God, and do not let sorrow capture your soul.

This is the weight of prophetic promises. they come with responsibilities. when God speaks a word over your life, it is not just a feel-good moment. it is a call to action. it is a call to align yourself with that word, to position yourself for its fulfillment. but too often, we treat prophetic words like lottery tickets, we get excited about the possibility, but we do not do the work to claim the prize. And the enemy is always waiting in the wings with a counterfeit. He is got alternatives that look good on the surface but are really just traps designed to derail you from God is plan. that is why discernment is so crucial. That is why we need to be in constant communication with God, not just receiving his words but seeking his guidance on how to walk them out.

The blessing of God is powerful. it is not just about material prosperity; it is about a fullness of life that can withstand the attacks of sorrow. but we have got to be wise in how we steward that blessing. we cannot get impatient and try to force God is hand like Sarah did. We cannot compromise and bring in elements from our old life in Egypt, thinking there will somehow speed up God is plan.

No, we have got to trust in the integrity of God is word. we have got to believe that if he said it, he will do it and in the meantime, we have got to keep our hearts pure, keep our minds focused, and keep our hands busy doing the work he is called us to do, because that is how we position ourselves for the fulfillment of those prophetic promises. That is how we ensure that when the blessing comes, it comes without sorrow attached. I challenge you to not just sit on those prophetic words you have received. do not just wait passively for them to come to pass. engage with God. ask him what you need to do to align yourself with his promises. and then, get to work. because the weight of prophetic promises is matched only by the weight of our responsibility to steward them well.

Restoration Of The Blessing

Suddenly, God showed up in Genesis 17. After what seems like an eternity of silence for Abaraham. About 24 long years after he and Sarah made that monumental mistake back in chapter 16. Can you even begin to imagine what those years must have been like for them? The doubt, the regret, the wondering if they'd completely ruined God is plan, it must have been excruciating.

But then, just when they probably thought all hope was lost, God makes His grand entrance. And let me tell you, He does not just tiptoe in, He comes in with a message to Abraham saying,

> *"Alright, Abraham, I have been waiting all this time for you to come to Me, to ask Me what it would take to see this promise through. But you never did. So now, I am here to lay it all out for you, and let me warn you – it is not going to be easy. There is going to be pain involved, but oh, the gain that comes after... it is going to be beyond anything you can imagine."*

I want you to really let this sink in, because I believe with that this message is not just for Abraham. It is for you and me, right here, right now. There are some of us (and you might be one of them) whose purpose on this Earth is so monumentally significant that God cannot afford to let us just coast through life. Those delays you have been experiencing, those heartbreaks that have left you reeling, the pain that is kept you up at night, it is not because God has forgotten about you or abandoned you. No, it is precisely because of how crucial your role is in the plan of God.

I know. As I am saying this, you might be thinking, *"Come on, that is a bit much. How can my little life be that important?"* But let me challenge you to shift your perspective for a moment. What if and this is a big what if, what if the very things that have been breaking your heart are actually preparing you for a breakthrough that is going to change not just your life, but the lives of others? What if God is allowing you to go through this refiner's fire because He knows that on the other side, you are going to emerge as a powerful instrument in His hands?

God is speaking to us, just as He spoke to Abraham, saying,

> *"Listen, what I am about to do through your life is so significant, so earth-shattering, that you cannot rely on what you see with your physical eyes alone. I am telling you about the plans I have, and if you choose to follow My lead, even when it does not make sense, you are going to understand why all hell seemed to break loose against you. You are going to see why I allowed you to walk through valleys so deep you thought you'd never see the light again. It is because I am about to use your life to tell a story so profound, so impactful, that it is going to echo through eternity."*

So, God shows up and essentially says,

> *"Abraham, I have been waiting all these years for you to come to Me, to ask Me what it would take to see this promise fulfilled. I have blessed you with silver and gold, with flocks and herds, but not once did you stop to ask Me, 'Lord, what's the cost of seeing this baby You promised come into the world?' And now here you are, 99 years old, and we are just getting to the heart of the matter."*

Then God tells Abraham that he needs to be circumcised. Now, pause for a moment. We are talking about a 99-year-old man being told he needs to undergo a painful, potentially dangerous procedure. But it is not just about the physical act. It is about what that act represents in the spiritual realm.

As God is laying out this covenant, He is simultaneously reaffirming His promise. Look at Genesis 17:6,

"I will give you millions of descendants."

Imagine the magnitude of this? He is speaking these words of abundance, of multiplicative blessing, to a man who's pushing a century in age, whose wife is 89, whose hope of ever having a child has long since withered away. From a human standpoint, everything about this situation screams *"impossible."* Abraham's body is old and tired, Sarah's womb is as good as dead, their bank of faith is running on empty but in the midst of all this apparent death, God is promise stands vibrant and alive.

"I will give you..." this is stark contrast to the reality he saw around him. And it was not just about having a child anymore. God was painting a picture of a legacy that would span generations, of kings rising from Abraham's lineage. It is as if God was saying,

"Abraham, I know what you see. I know what logic tells you. But I am asking you to see beyond the natural, to tap into a realm where My word trumps every law of nature."

In verse 7, God adds another layer to this covenant. He is not just promising descendants; He is promising to be their God, to establish an everlasting covenant with them. This is huge, folks. God is basically saying,

> *"I am not just interested in giving you a son, Abraham. I am interested in building a relationship that will transcend generations, that will impact nations, that will change the course of human history."*

God just reveal it now, after years of promising Abraham a child. It is as if God is saying, *"Now we have an agreement."* But why now? Why not earlier? I believe it is because God wanted Abraham to reach a point where he understood that this was not just about having a baby. It was about entering into a deep, binding, permanent relationship with the Creator of the universe. Circumcision, in this context, represents so much more than a physical act. It is a cutting away of the flesh, a visible, irreversible sign of commitment to God is covenant. In the spiritual sense, it is about cutting away our reliance on our own strength, our own wisdom, our own timing. It is about saying, *"God, I am all in. I am surrendering everything to You, even the parts of me that I have held onto most tightly."*

There are certain things God likes to take care of in our lives before He releases the fullness of His blessing. When God removes sorrow, when He heals those deep wounds in our hearts, when He aligns our spirits with His purpose that is when the blessing becomes truly enjoyable. But when a blessing meets unresolved sorrow or bitterness, it can become tasteless, even burdensome.

How many times have you seen people receive the very thing they have been praying for, only to find that it does not bring the joy or satisfaction they expected? That is often because there is inner work that needs to be done, heart issues that need to be addressed, before we can fully embrace and appreciate God is blessings. Let me show you something about God is timing and preparation.

Abraham had to waited 25 years from the time God first promised him a son to the moment Isaac was born. That is a quarter of a century of waiting, hoping, probably doubting at times. But during that time, God was not idle. He was working on Abraham's character, his faith, his understanding of who God is. God is not just interested in giving us things. He is interested in shaping us into people who can handle those things, who can steward His blessings well. Sometimes, the very delays we experience are God is way of preparing us for the weight of the blessing He wants to entrust to us.

This pattern repeats throughout Scripture and, I believe, in our own lives as well. The question is, are you willing to embrace the process? Are you willing to trust God even when His timing does not align with yours, even when the path He is leading you on seems to be taking you further away from your dreams rather than closer to them? There is something profound about the way God dealt with Abraham. He did not just give him a son, He gave him a new name, a new identity. He transformed him from Abram *("exalted father")* to Abraham *("father of many")*. God was essentially saying, *"I am not just changing your circumstances; I am changing who you are completely."* And is not that what we all long for? Not just for your situations to change, but for you to be transformed from the inside out? To become people who can look at impossible situations and see them through God is eyes of possibility? To have the kind of faith that can move mountains, not because of your own strength, but because you have learned to tap into God is unlimited power?

This is what God has prepared for each of us on. It is not an easy one. It will likely involve times of waiting, times of pain, times when we feel like you are walking in complete darkness. But if you can hold onto the truth that God is working even when you cannot see it, if you can trust that He is preparing you for something far greater than you could ever imagine, then you can find strength to persevere. The very trials you are facing right now could be the training ground for your destiny. The delays that frustrate you, the setbacks that discourage you, the pain that threatens to overwhelm you all of these could be part of God is process of preparing you for a purpose that will impact generations.

When God spoke to Abraham about his descendants, He was not just talking about a biological legacy. He was talking about a spiritual legacy, about people who would carry the light of God is truth into a dark world. And I believe He is speaking the same thing over many of us today. You might feel like Abraham did, old, tired, past your prime, wondering if you have missed your chance. But as long as you have breath in your lungs, it is not too late for God to do something miraculous through your life. Your age, your past mistakes, your current circumstances, none of these can limit what God wants to do in and through you. But here are you willing to pay the price? Are you willing to undergo the spiritual circumcision God might be calling you to? Are you ready to cut away the things that are holding you back, the self-reliance, the pride, the fear, the bitterness? Are you willing to enter into a covenant relationship with God that will change everything?

Because make no mistake, when God shows up like He did with Abraham, when He starts speaking about covenants and promises, He is not just talking about tweaking your life a little bit. He is talking about a complete overhaul, a total transformation that will affect every area of your existence. It is not always going to be comfortable. In fact, it might be downright painful at times. But I can promise you this, the pain of remaining the same will always be greater than the pain of change. The discomfort of stepping out in faith will pale in comparison to the regret of playing it safe and missing out on God is best for your life.

CHAPTER THREE

WALKING OR MINING THE BLESSING

You know, I used to have this notion and I bet many of you did too that when God is blessing shows up, it just swoops in and gobbles up all our sorrows, neat and tidy, like a cosmic vacuum cleaner. But oh, how wrong I was! The Lord has been opening my eyes to a deeper truth, and let me tell you, it is revolutionary.

There exists a caliber of blessing, a magnitude so immense, that when God decides to unleash it into someone's life, it does not just casually stroll in, no, it comes crashing like a tidal wave, a spiritual tsunami if you will. It does not merely swallow up your sorrow as I once thought. No, it does something far more powerful, far more transformative. This blessing, when it hits, it flushes out sorrow. Yes! It is not about absorption; it is about total expulsion.

I want you to really get this. When a blessing swallows' sorrow, what happens? The sorrow becomes part of the blessing's makeup, does not it? It is like mixing bitter herbs into a sweet cake, sure, you might not taste the bitterness as strongly, but it is still there, altering the flavor, becoming part of the nutrients, as it were. And this, my friends, is where so many believers have found themselves entangled in all sorts of complications. They have been operating under this misguided belief that it is okay for their blessings to simply mask their sorrows, to cover them up like a band-aid over a festering wound.

But God is been showing me that He is got something far better in mind for us. He is not in the business of camouflaging our pain; He wants to flush it out completely, to create a clean slate where His blessings can truly flourish without the lingering aftertaste of past sorrows. Do not get me wrong. God, in His infinite wisdom and sovereignty, might allow some folks' blessings to swallow up their sorrows for a season. But we need to understand that this is not the ultimate goal. It is like that parable of the wheat and the tares that Jesus spoke about in Matthew 13. A man plants good seed in his field, but while everyone is sleeping, an enemy sneaks in and sows' weeds among the wheat. When the plants sprout, the owner's servants are all in a tizzy, wanting to yank out those weeds right away. But what does the owner say? *"Let them grow together until the harvest."*

This parable gives us a glimpse into the permissive will of God. He allows things to coexist for a time, the good and the bad, the blessings and the curses, all intertwined like some cosmic double helix (I will explain this more soon). And let me tell you, this creates one wild ride of a life for many believers. You have got money flowing in, praise God! But right alongside it, there is a health crisis nipping at your heels. You are experiencing breakthroughs in your career, hallelujah! But at the same time, your family's falling apart at the seams. It is like your life's become this spiritual rollercoaster, one minute you are shouting from the mountaintop, the next you are scraping yourself off the valley floor. You are simultaneously the poster child for God is goodness and the cautionary tale of Satan's schemes. It is exhausting, is not it? Testimonies and tragedies, all growing together in the field of your life.

I need you to understand that the purpose of God is blessing in our lives goes way beyond just accumulating stuff, cars, houses, bank accounts bursting at the seams. Do not get me wrong, those things are great, and God does want to prosper us. But the blessing He has in mind is so much more expansive, so much more transformative than we often realize. This blessing God wants to pour out, it is got layers upon layers of goodness to add to your life. You have got to work it. Yes, you heard me right. God is blessing is not just going to fall into your lap while you sit back and twiddle your thumbs. No, sir! You have got to engage with it, cultivate it, mine it for all it is worth.

And let me tell you, this process of working the blessing, it is not for the faint of heart. It requires discernment, patience, and a willingness to be selective. It is like God is original instructions to the Israelites about farming. He laid down some specific rules. *"Do not plant different crops in the same field,"* He said. *"Keep your grain separate from your corn, your millet distinct from your guinea corn."* Why would God be so particular about agricultural practices? Because He is trying to teach us something profound about how to steward His blessings in our lives. He wants our lives to be distinct, clearly defined, not a jumbled mess of competing priorities and mixed messages.

When harvest time rolls around, God does not want you scratching your head, trying to figure out what's what in the field of your life. He wants you to have clarity, to know exactly what you are reaping and when. Today, you are harvesting health. Tomorrow, it is wealth. The day after, it is influence in your business or your political sphere. Each blessing distinct, each harvest unique. This is why God told the Israelites not to sow other crops in the rows of their vineyards. He even added a pretty serious consequence, if they did, both the crops and the grapes would be confiscated by the priest.

God is serious about us keeping our blessings distinct and pure. And this is what it means to walk in the blessing. It is not passive; it is active. It is not just about receiving; it is about engaging. Every experience, every challenge, every seeming setback is potentially a rich vein of blessing if you know how to mine it properly.

The Office Of The Priest

One of the primary assignments of the priest and I am not just talking about the ones in the Old Testament, but also about those who stand in that priestly role in our lives today is to legislate on our behalf. What does that even mean? Well, it is twofold, and each aspect is as important as the other.

First, the priest's job is to instruct us. they are there to impart wisdom, to help us understand God is ways, to guide us through the intricate maze of spiritual truths that can often seem overwhelming. Think about it, how many times have you found yourself scratching your head, trying to make sense of a particular scripture or a spiritual principle that just seems beyond your grasp? You need a priest. They are the spiritual teachers, that will break down truths into bite-sized pieces that you can digest and apply.

The second part of their legislative role is equally important; they stand and look. Now, you might be thinking, *"What's so special about standing and looking? I can do that!"* But this is not just casual observation I am talking about. This is spiritual vigilance of the highest order. The priest stands as a watchman on the walls, constantly scanning the spiritual horizon for potential threats, discerning the times and seasons, and alerting us to both dangers and opportunities that we might otherwise miss.

I started saying earlier, that God instructs the children of Israel specifically about farming. He said, *"Do not sow things together."* Now, why would God be so particular about agricultural practices? Because He is trying to teach something important about how to steward our spiritual lives. if God said not to sow things together, then who on earth (or should I say, who from hell) does the devil think he is, that will want to plant sorrow in your life? And that is why I am walking this truth gradually into your spirit. I want you to grasp it fully, to let it sink deep into your bones. Because

I believe with every fiber of my being that by the Spirit of God, through this book, every sorrow that is been attached to your life is going to be eliminated in the name of Jesus.

But here is the thing and this is crucial; you have got to be sensitive in the spirit. You cannot just bumble through life, oblivious to the spiritual realities around you. You need to sharpen your spiritual senses, to develop that keen discernment that allows you to identify what's of God and what's not. Because, as the Bible tells us, even when the good man plants his seed, and men goes to sleep. And sleep, my friends, is a legitimate thing. We all need rest; we cannot be on high alert 24/7. But it is in those moments of legitimate rest that the enemy tries to sneak in and take advantage. He is always looking for an opportunity to plant his seed, to make his presence known in our lives.

I know you might be thinking. *"what, if I spot something that is not of God, shouldn't I just rip it out immediately?"* And that is a natural response. It is like the disciples of Jesus who, when they saw the tares growing among the wheat, were all gung-ho about taking immediate action. *"Let's do something now, now!"* they said. But Jesus, in His infinite wisdom, said, *"No."* And there is a profound lesson for us here.

You see, when it comes to annihilating sorrow from our lives, you have got to be wise. you cannot just go in guns blazing, trying to annihilate every negative thing you see. Because if you are not careful, in that zealous attempt to get rid of the bad, you might end up destroying the blessing too. It is like trying to perform delicate surgery with a sledgehammer, you might remove the tumor, but you will cause a whole lot of collateral damage in the process.

That is why I am urging you, with all the passion in my heart, to uncloud your hearts. You need to create space for the revelation of truth to penetrate deep. Because if your heart is crowded, if it is cluttered with all sorts of distractions and competing priorities, it is going to be incredibly difficult for the revelation of truth to make a real difference in your life.

Let's look at what Jesus said in Matthew 6:20-21 (The Passion Translation):

> *"Instead, stockpile heavenly treasures for yourselves that cannot be stolen and will never rust, decay, or lose their value. For your heart will always pursue what you value as treasure."*

The eyes of your spirit, that is what allows revelation light to flood into your being. If your heart is unclouded, if it is open and receptive, then that light can come pouring in like a tidal wave of divine illumination.

And let me tell you, that light is seeking to flood in. It is not playing hard to get; it is not hiding from you. No, it is actively trying to penetrate your hearts and minds. Why? So that as you journey through this crazy, mixed-up life, you can look at your circumstances, your relationships, your challenges, and your victories, and tell the difference. You can say with confidence, *"Oh, this right here? This is wheat. But that over there? That is tares."*

The Master said, *"Do not take it out; let them grow together."* Now, that does not sound like the best plan. Shouldn't we be getting rid of anything that is not of God as soon as we spot it? And you are right; it is not the ideal scenario. But given the situation at hand, wisdom is profitable to direct. Sometimes, the wisest course of action is not the most obvious or the most satisfying in the short term. Wisdom demands that we should not, in our overzealous attempt to eliminate sorrow, end up destroying the blessing in the process. It is a delicate balance, a spiritual tightrope walk that requires discernment, patience, and yes, sometimes even the willingness to let things be for a season.

There was this old king who, by God is grace, became one of my converts. Now, this was not just any old convert, this was a Muslim who had made the pilgrimage to Mecca not once, not twice, but three times. I am talking about an 80-year-old man deeply entrenched in his faith and cultural traditions. As a young preacher, fresh-faced and full of zeal, I had my heart set on the day this king would publicly declare his faith in Christ. In my naive enthusiasm, I believed that through him, the entire village would come flocking to our church. I had visions of our little congregation becoming the biggest in town overnight. So, I prayed, oh how I prayed! *"Oh God,"* I will cry out, *"let this king identify with You publicly!"*

We would make regular visits to the king, and he'd graciously send people out to attend to us so we could pray for him. And in my young, inexperienced mind, I kept thinking, *"Imagine if this one man came to church! The whole town would follow suit!"* Looking back now, I can see how foolish that thinking was. But you know what? Not all foolishness is wrong; sometimes it is just a sign that we are not yet mature or experienced enough to see the bigger picture. In my youthful exuberance, I failed to consider the potential disaster that could unfold if this man, popularly known as a devout Muslim, suddenly showed up at our church. I did not stop to think about how the towns people might react to their respected leader, whom they had collectively sent to Mecca multiple times to be a good Muslim and govern them well, suddenly embracing a faith brought by some young, unknown preacher who had just arrived in town.

But there I was, my young mind filled with visions of grandeur, looking forward to the day the Oba (that is what we call the king) would come to church. I could almost taste the sweet victory of sending a report to my spiritual fathers, proclaiming, *"Glory to God! You sent us to this village, and now the whole place is revived! Everyone in town, just like the Apostle Paul, has been transformed. The king and all the villagers are now members of our church!"*

So, driven by this burning desire to see immediate results, I decided to take matters into my own hands. I prayed fervently, waiting for a vision from God to tell me when the right time would be to invite the Oba to church. But when no vision came, do you know what I did? I gave myself a vision. That is right, I convinced myself that it was time, that God must surely want me to extend this invitation now. With my heart pounding with anticipation, I made my way to the Oba's palace. *"Baba,"* I said, using the respectful term for an elder, *"I know you have been born again now for all these months. Do not you think it would be good for you to come to church? Who knows? Maybe through your salvation, other people will also come to Christ!"*

What happened next is something I will never forget. This old, wise man looked at me with patience in his eyes, and he began to speak to me in a parable. *"My son,"* he said, his voice rich with years of wisdom, *"if a mosquito bites you and is sucking your blood, you will smack it hard and kill it right?"* I nodded eagerly, agreeing with his statement but having no idea where he was going with this analogy. He continued, *"But what happens if that same mosquito is biting you on your eye and is sucking your blood? Will you kill it with the same intensity you used to kill the one on your thigh?"* I stood there, a bit confused, as he went on, *"The wisest thing is not to kill the mosquito here. Even if it is biting you, you must allow it to suck your blood and just do whatever you can do to let the mosquito escape. Otherwise, you will need a doctor to fix your eye."*

In that moment, I felt like someone had just added 20 years to my life. The wisdom of his words hit me like a tidal wave, washing away my naive enthusiasm and replacing it with a deeper understanding of the complexities of spiritual leadership. *"Let the mosquito escape,"* he said, *"otherwise, you will be eyeless because you were trying to kill a mosquito."*

I was, thinking I had it all figured out, ready to charge ahead with my grand plans for revival. But this wise old king, with a simple parable about a mosquito, had just opened my eyes to a much deeper truth. He went on to explain, *"You know, if I go to church now, the entire village may not come to worship God; they may come and destroy the church."* And there it was the harsh reality that my youthful enthusiasm had failed to consider. In my eagerness to see immediate results, to eliminate what I perceived as the *"sorrow"* of the king's public Muslim identity, I had almost invited disaster upon the very church I was trying to grow. Sometimes, in our attempt to eliminate sorrow, we end up destroying the very blessing we are trying to nurture.

CHAPTER FOUR

WHAT KIND OF BLESSING MUST WE TARGET?

T he blessing that comes like a flood, the one that overflows. It is the blessing that flushes out sorrow. This is the kind of blessing we must set our sights on, not a trickle, but a torrent that sweeps away all traces of sadness and fills our lives with abundance. Initially, one might assume Jesus was addressing mortal laborers, instructing them on patience and discernment. However, He was referring to angels, celestial harvesters tasked with the divine mission of separating good from evil, joy from sorrow. This revelation opens up an entirely new perspective on how blessings operate in our lives.

This supernatural process of eliminating sorrow is not something we can orchestrate through human logic or effort alone. It requires our spiritual hearts to be wide open, receptive to the divine orchestrations happening beyond our natural sight. When our hearts are open, our minds steady, and we resolve to enjoy everything God has for us, we position ourselves to receive blessings that defy human understanding. To fully embrace this flood of blessings, we must make a conscious decision not to give the devil any power or license to operate in our lives. We cannot allow the enemy to manipulate, slow down, or destroy what God is doing. It is about standing firm in our faith, declaring with every fiber of our being that we will not be moved from our position of blessing, regardless of the circumstances that may swirl around us.

Jesus' words about gathering the wheat carry a serious implication for our spiritual lives. To experience the proliferating power of blessing, we must be willing to engage in a thorough spiritual house-cleaning. This involves identifying and uprooting the *"tares"* in our lives, those thoughts, habits, relationships and influences that threaten to choke out the good seed God has planted within us. You must take time to ensure these tares and sources of sorrow are gathered and forcefully tied in bundles to be burned.

As a wise master builder, I feel compelled to prepare you for what lies ahead. The assignments God has entrusted to you are precious, and I have prayed fervently that they will never die in your hands. I am not just praying words; it is a spiritual investment in your future, a declaration of faith in the potential God has placed within you. These prayers do not stop there. I am acutely aware that our obedience to God often comes at a cost, not just to ourselves but to those around us. As we align ourselves more closely with God is will, it can create ripples that affect our relationships, our schedules, and our priorities. With this in mind, I have extended my prayers to cover those whose lives might be momentarily disrupted by our pursuit of God is calling.

This brings to mind my own experiences as a father, trying to strike the delicate balance between my divine calling and my responsibilities to my family. There are countless times when the demands of ministry have pulled me away from precious moments with my children. The desire to be there for every milestone, every laugh, every tear is strong. Of course, I always make time for my family, do not get me wrong. God accepts me; I am a great father, and I know that. But there are times when I long to just close up the office early, pick them up from school, and take them out for ice cream.

One of the blessings God gave me is to provide me with a good father and a good mother. My father, in particular, exemplified a beautiful balance of strength and tenderness, discipline and joy. I recall with vivid fondness the anticipation we felt as children, waiting for him to return home. We would even bribe each other to stay awake, promising to share our *"suya"* (grilled beef) if someone would wake us when Daddy came home. My father's presence never threatened or scared us; instead, it brought an atmosphere of love and celebration.

The rituals of our family life were more than just routines. They were moments of connection and joy that have greatly shaped my understanding of fatherhood and blessing. Sharing meals, sipping from our parents' glasses (a practice steeped in the culture of our time), dancing to the music from his prized LPs, these experiences created a foundation of security and love that has influenced my life.

He was the wildest lion I have ever known and yet the gentlest lamb, tender with us. He was a warrior, a champion, a heavy-duty provider who ensured we had everything we needed. Yet he was also incredibly kind and patient with us kids. I saw all these qualities, and I knew I was going to be a good father. I saw love, I saw patience, and I witnessed firsthand how to balance strength with tenderness.

Imagine now that I have a call from God, I strive to embody all that I learned from my father to my children. Though there are times when work demands keep me away, I am always there in spirit. God has blessed me with children who are very understanding, and because of that, we have a very healthy relationship.

The Cost Of Obedience And The Power Of Intercessory Prayer

Obedience to God, it is not no walk in the park. It comes with a price tag, and I am not talking about no small change either. The cost is not just on you, but it spreads out, which touches the lives of those around you like ripples in a pond. That is why I have been hammering this message into my pastors' heads: if your parents are alive and still breathing, you better be praying for them like your life depends on it. because in a way, it does.

Now, you might be saying, *"But I am not in a position to take care of anybody right now."* Listen here, and listen well. That does not matter one bit when it comes to prayer. You might not have two nickels to rub together, but you have got a direct line to the Almighty, and that is worth more than all the gold in Fort Knox. So, you pray. You pray for those you are supposed to be takin' care of, even if right now all you can offer is your words lifted up to heaven.

It does not matter if you are the baby of the family or the middle born. If God is called you, and that anointing is on your head, then you best be stepping up to the plate. You have got to embrace that responsibility of being the spiritual father (or mother) of your family. It is not about birth order no more; it is about who's answering the call.

Now, I want you to expand your prayer circle. Do not just stop at your immediate family. Pray for your loved ones, every last one of them. If you have got children, you better be covering them in prayers. And do not you dare forget about your pastors too. These men and women are pouring out their lives for you, laboring in the Word and in prayer. They need your spiritual support just as much as you need theirs.

But where the rubber meets the road. I want you to pray for anyone and I mean anyone, whose life is paying part of the price for your obedience to God. You heard me right. Your walk with God, your answer to His call, it is got a ripple effect. Some folks might be feeling the squeeze because you are following God is path. So, what do you do? You pray that God will compensate them. Pray that He will reward them in ways you cannot even imagine. Ask Him to bless them so abundantly that their cups are overflowing. Pray for their prosperity, that there will have more than enough to meet their needs and then some.

But do not stop there. Pray for their protection. Ask God to put a hedge of protection around them so strong that the devil himself cannot break through. Pray that they will not become a distraction to you in your walk with God. Now, I know that might sound harsh, but hear me out. Sometimes, the enemy will use the people closest to us to try and pull us off course. So, we got to pray that God will keep them safe and secure, but also that He will keep them from becoming stumbling blocks in our path. Pray that the health of your parents will not become a distraction to you, and pray that God will cause them to live long.

If a person's time on this earth is drawing to a close, sometimes it is better for them to go home to glory than to linger here in pain and suffering. Now, do not get me wrong. I am not telling you to pray for your parents to die. That is not what I am saying at all. But if they have lived a long, full life, if they are up there in years and their health is failing, it is okay to accept that maybe, just maybe, it is time for them to rest.

Billy Graham got to a point where he was ready to go home. He kept talking about seeing Ruth again, about how he couldn't wait to be reunited with his beloved wife in heaven. There is a beauty in that, a peace that comes from knowing you have run your race and you are ready for that final rest. So, if your parents are getting on in years, especially if they are pushing 90 or beyond, it is okay to pray,

> "Lord, Your will be done. If it is their time to come home, let them go peacefully. Do not let them become a burden or a liability. Let them finish strong and enter into their rest." But always, always pray for long life. Say: "My parents will live long, healthy, blessed lives in Jesus' name!"

Secondly. I want you to pray for your congregation, for every single member of your church (if you are pastor). Pray that God will show up in their lives in ways so miraculous it'll make the nightly news look boring. Pray that the faithful ones, the ones who've been sticking it out through thick and thin, will become walking, talking testimonies. You know what I am talking about, the kind of testimonies that spread like wildfire, that get people talking and give glory to God.

Let me tell you about a sister in our church. She is 71 years of age, and God give her a testimony that is got everybody talking. As she is preparing for retirement, God is opened up doors she never even knew existed. That is the kind of thing we need to be praying for. We need to be asking God to give our loves one testimonies so astounding that people cannot help but sit up and take notice. That is exactly what God wants. He is itching to bless His people, but He is waiting on you. Yes, you! You are the priest, the intercessor. God is waiting for you to give Him permission to move in mighty ways. So do not hold back in your prayers. Ask big, believe big, and watch God do big things.

But we cannot forget about the unfaithful ones either. Pray that there will have a life-changing encounter with God. Pray that there will experience Christ in such a powerful way that there will never be the same. Cause let me tell you something, Christ is not too happy with unfaithful people. The Bible's clear on this: *"He that is faithful in little, much will be given to him."* some of us are serving right now, but you are not being faithful in the little things. Listen up, because this is important. At some point in your life, God is going to give you much. But if you have not learned to be faithful with the little, that *"much"* is going to break you down instead of building you up. It is when you have got plenty that you really see whether you have been serving God rightly or not.

It is easy to go to your 9-to-5 job, collect your paycheck, and bad-mouth your boss. Then you get this idea that God is called you to start your own business. Well, go ahead and try it. But do not be surprised if two years down the line, you are struggling to get even one client. See, if you are faithful in your current job, if you give it your all and honor God in your work, you will be amazed at how fruitful you can be. Take the owner of Mariano's for example. That man succeeded because he was faithful even when he was just an employee. He is not the first person to leave a job or get fired and try to start his own company. Many have tried and failed. But the faithful ones? They are still shining bright. And let me tell you something, you will shine too if you learn to be faithful!

Jesus said He'd tell His reapers, His harvesters, to take out the bad ones first. As we deal with sorrow and hardship, He said they'd prepare it to be burned. Then they'd harvest the wheat that is the good stuff and put it in His barn. What's He saying? God is going to separate the sorrow from your life. The fire of God is going to burn up every bit of sorrow, every scrap of pain and disappointment. And every blessing that comes your way? It is going to be separated out, stored up in God is barn, lasting from generation to generation.

This is not just talk. This is going to reflect in every area of your life, your health, your business, your career. It is all going to be touched by God is separating fire and His storehouse of blessings. That is why God is put it on my heart to tell you: do not you dare get weary. Do not you dare get tired. And whatever you do, do not you dare be afraid. Even if it feels like all hell's broken loose against you, even if it seems like everything's falling apart, you hold on.

The Bible tells us that when men slept, the enemy came and sowed tares. It might feel like the enemy's planted something nasty in the middle of all your hard work and effort. But listen to me, God is about to eliminate every bit of sorrow. When His blessings come, they are going to come like a flood, washing away every trace of sorrow. And your blessings? They are going to grow and multiply, blessing upon blessing, favor upon favor, grace upon grace.

You might say, *"But pastor, it feels like every time I take one step forward, I get knocked two steps back."* Maybe you got a new job, and the next thing you know, the doctor's giving you some scary news. I heard about a member of our church who had everything going well, and then out of nowhere, the doctor drops a bomb on them. Life can be challenging, no doubt about it.

But let me tell you something, child of God. I know what God said to me, and I am passing it on to you. He said every tare in your life, every weed, every problem, every setback is going to be burnt up by His fire. That pillar of fire we read about in Exodus? It is not done doing its job. You are going to watch as your life gets purified by the fire of God. And after the fire comes the harvest. God said, *"Then they will harvest the wheat and put it into my barn."* What does that mean for you? It means God is going to preserve your progress. He is going to protect your achievements. He is going to secure your prosperity in the name of Jesus.

You know, that was Abraham's big fear. He was obedient, he was following God, but he did not have a son. He was worried, wondering, *"How am I going to achieve all this if I do not have an heir?"* But God reassured him. He said, *"Abraham, I am going to give you more children than you can count. Your descendants are going to be as numerous as the stars in the sky."*

That is the kind of God we serve. A God who sees beyond our current circumstances, who has plans for us that are bigger than anything we could dream up on our own. So, when you are praying, when you are interceding for others, remember this: you are not just changing their lives, you are changing your own. You are aligning yourself with God is purposes, and in doing so, you are opening yourself up to blessings you cannot even imagine.

CHAPTER FIVE

CONTENDING FOR
THE BLESSING

◆ ◆ ◆

Isaiah 59:19: "…when the enemy comes in like a flood, the Spirit of the Lord shall lift up a standard against them."

N ow, most of us have been quoting this verse like this. But let me tell you something that is not the way it is supposed to be read. We have been missing the mark, and it is time to hit the bullseye.

The Living Bible translation gives more sense. It says,

> *"Then at last they will reverence and glorify the name of God from west to east; for He will come like a flood driven by Jehovah."*

Now, I know some of y'all did not catch that, so let me break it down for you. This is saying that people from one end of the earth to the other are going to fear the Lord and respect His glory. And when He shows up? It is going to be no gentle trickle. No sir! He is coming like a fast-flowing river, pushed along by the very breath of God Himself.

But wait, there is more! The Message translation takes it even further. It says,

> "Even the far-off islands will get paid off in full. In the west, they will fear the name of God; in the east, they will fear the glory of God, for He will arrive like a river in flood stage, whipped to a torrent by the wind of God."

Can you feel that? That is power, my friends. That is the kind of force that changes things and destinies.

The King James Version has led us astray on this one. It is got us thinking that when the enemy comes like a flood, that is when the Spirit of God raises a standard. But that is not how it is supposed to be written. That is not the true meaning of this verse. If you really want to get to the heart of it, you can look at the Tree of Life Version. That is where you will find the purest Hebrew interpretation. And let me tell you, it is going to change the way you see this scripture forever.

See, the enemy is coming we know that. But what's going to make people from east to west sit up and take notice? What's going to make them fear and respect the name of God and His glory? It is how God shocks them when they show up thinking they can come against His people. When it talks about a flood, it is not talking about the enemy. No sir! That flood? That is the Holy Spirit Himself! When the enemy comes sneaking around, it is the Holy Spirit that rises up like a flood. It is the wind of God that is going to flush out every last one of those sorrows.

Any sorrow that is been camping out in your life, any trouble that is been hanging around. It is about to get washed away by the flood of God. Whatever pain you have been carrying, whatever heartache you have been nursing the flood of the Holy Spirit is coming to wash it all away. So, lift up your head and get ready, because your season of joy is on its way!

Let me hit you with the Tree of Life Version one more time:

> *"So, from the west, they will fear the name of Adonai, Lord and Master, and His glory from the rising of the sun, for He will come like a rushing stream driven along by Ruach Adonai."*

Now, for those who do not know, Ruach is the Hebrew word for wind, and it is also the name for the Holy Spirit. I am talking about the moving wind, the intelligent wind, the roaring wind. Ruach Adonai that is the Spirit of the Lord and Master, coming to sweep away every obstacle in your path.

I will soon show you how to identify the presence of sorrow and the kind of blessings that annihilates sorrow. There are things that can happen to a person sometimes that just one blessing is enough to defeat your sorrow. Esau cried and begged his father for a blessing. He said, *"I do not care what you gave my brother; I just need one blessing. because if you give me just one, I know how to work that blessing till it wipes out all my sorrow."* But his father, Isaac, had to tell him, *"Son, I gave it all to your brother."* And Esau, he couldn't believe it. He said, *"Do not you have even one left for me? Just one?"*

See, Esau had been careless. He lived his life without thinking about the consequences, and when it came time for him to make sense of his life, all that carelessness and wickedness caught up with him. He cried out,

"Father, do not you have even one blessing left for me? Oh my father, bless me too!" (Genesis 27:39-40)

Isaac says: *"Yours will be a life of sorrow, not one of ease and luxury, but you shall earn your way with your sword."* Can you imagine? Everything Esau was going to get in life; he'd have to fight for. No easy street for him. No sir. It was going to be a life of sorrow, not ease and luxury. Now, I do not know what took the blessing from you. Maybe it was not stolen by a person; maybe it was stolen by the grave. Perhaps the father or mother or the voice that was supposed to speak that blessing over your life died before they ever got the chance. And now you are sitting there, wishing that the blessing that was never spoken is somehow working for you. It does not work that way. Blessings cannot just be wished into existence. They got to be declared, proclaimed, and invoked. That is why they have to be provoked to be invoked. Isaac knew this. That is why he told Jacob, *"I need you to provoke the blessing."* Esau wasted his time, but Jacob? He found a way to provoke that blessing, and Isaac invoked it on him.

Isaac told Esau, *"You have to earn your way with your sword; for a time, you will serve your brother, but you will finally shake loose from him and be free."*

Can you imagine the heartbreak? That is why Esau cried out, *"Papa, I need just one blessing."* But Isaac had to tell him, *"I gave it all to your brother."* if there is such a thing as *"all"* when it comes to blessings, then I am declaring right now that you will receive it all! Every last drop of blessing that God has for you is coming your way.

If Esau could shake loose from sorrow, then you better believe you can be free from it too. All those repeated sicknesses in your body? They are not of God. Some of you are entertaining infirmity like it is a welcome guest. But that is not no way to live! Life is better lived rough if you can bounce back like a stone. And as long as you do not believe what I am saying, you will never enjoy the fullness of what God has for you.

Let me ask you, are you not happier when you are healthy? Every time you check your account, it is in the red. The money you are spending on overdraft fees is more than what you make in two days of work. That is not God is plan for you! But I have good news, if you find yourself in that situation, this blessing brings you out.

See, we serve a God of abundance, a God who wants to see His children prosper in every area of life. He is not interested in seeing you scrape by, living paycheck to paycheck. No, He wants to see you thrive, to see you walking in such abundance that you become a blessing to others. You have to position yourself to receive. You have to be ready to contend for that blessing. Just like Jacob wrestled with God all night long, saying, *"I will not let you go until you bless me,"* you have to be willing to press in, to push through, to fight for what God has promised you.

The enemy is not going to roll out the red carpet for your blessing. He is going to fight you tooth and nail, trying to keep you bound in sorrow and lack. But that is where the flood comes in. That is where the Ruach Adonai, the Spirit of the Lord, comes rushing in like a mighty river, sweeping away every obstacle, every hindrance, every chain that is been holding you back. When God decides to bless you, there is no power in heaven or earth that can stop it. When He opens a door, no man can shut it. When He speaks a word over your life, it is as good as done. But you have to be ready to receive it. You have to be willing to step out in faith, to take hold of what God is offering you.

And let me tell you, when that blessing hits your life, it is going to change everything. It is going to turn your mourning into dancing, your sorrow into joy. It is going to take you from the pit to the palace, from the backside of the desert to the forefront of your destiny. But you cannot just sit there waiting for it to fall in your lap. You have to contend for it. You have to fight for it. You have to press in with everything you have got, believing that God is faithful to His word and that He is got nothing but good things in store for you.

God is not finished with you yet. He is got plans for you that are bigger than anything you could ever imagine. He is got blessings lined up for you that will make your head spin. But you have to be ready. You have to be willing. You have to be in a position to receive. I am challenging you today, stop accepting less than God is best for your life. Stop settling for sickness when God is promising your health. Stop living in lack when God is promising you abundance. It is time to rise up and take hold of everything

God has for you.

It is time to contend for the blessing. It is time to let the flood of God is Spirit wash away every trace of sorrow in your life. It is time to step into the fullness of your destiny, to walk in the abundance that God has promised you. You see, when that flood comes, when the Ruach Adonai starts moving in your life, no sorrow going to be able to stand. No lack is going to be able to hold on. No sickness is going to be able to keep its grip on you.

So, get ready. Get in position. because your season of blessing is on its way. The flood is coming, and it is going to change everything. Your time of sorrow is over. Your season of lack is done. Your days of struggling are coming to an end. The blessing is here, and it is got your name on it. Reach out and take hold of it. Contend for it with everything you have got.

Sorrow As A Sign Of Imminent Blessing

Genesis 17:15-16, and let me tell you, this is not any surface-level Sunday school lesson. This is the nitty-gritty of how God works in our lives, especially when it comes to sorrow and blessing.

God is said concerning Sarai, I will do a couple of things to her, and it is not just a name change. He is rewriting' her whole story. He says, *"Her name is no longer sorrow; her name is no longer poverty, sickness, lack and want, mistakes, errors, or foolish mistakes, avoidable mistakes."* Can you feel the weight of that? God is taking all the baggage, all the hurt, all the shame that Sarai's been carrying, and He is tossing it out the window.

God is about to address that whole Hagar situation. When Sarai got impatient and decided to *"help"* God out by giving her maid to Abraham. Yeah, that mess. God is saying, *"Take Hagar; let her give you the baby God promised you."* Now, do not get it twisted. This is not God endorsing their plan. He is acknowledging the mistake, but He is also saying, *"It is okay; we are going to correct that."* Verse 16 said: *"I will bless her."* All this time, God is been telling Abraham,

"I will bless you." And Abraham's been happy about it, sure. But he is also been wondering, *"How, God? How are you going to bless me when I am going it alone? I do not even have a kid to carry on my name!"*

And God, in His infinite wisdom and patience, says, *"Okay, you are going to have your own son."* Imagine the relief that must've washed over Abraham. He rushes back to Sarah, all excited, telling her, *"The Lord came to me in a vision and said I am going to have a son!"*

So, Sarah, bless her heart, thinks she is got it all figured out. She says, *"I have an idea! We are going to help God make this baby."* And just like that, she brings Hagar into the picture, not realizing she is bringing sorrow upon herself.

See, the sorrow Sarah was dealing with was not just about not having a child. It was the shame, the feeling that she was the reason Abraham was not fulfilling God is plan and purpose. She felt like she was the bad news in his life, so she was trying to bring some good news. But what she did not realize was that sorrow has a way of attaching itself to any place it senses a blessing coming.

Some of us have been facing some serious sorrow lately. Maybe it is hit you so hard you thought it was a sign that God had abandoned you. But I am here to tell you, that is not the case at all! That sorrow you have been facing? It is announcing that your blessing is closer than you ever thought possible.

God is sending a message loud and clear: This is not the time to get upset, weary, fearful, or foolish. It is time to look out for the God who gives songs in the night. The sorrow you saw before? It came to let you know that your blessing' is right around the corner. Those material things you have been praying for? They are so close you can almost touch them.

God is asking me to tell you to get ready because your blessing is not just going to swallow your sorrow. No, it is going to flush it out completely. This blessing is going to be so rich, so abundant in your life that there will not be any room left for sorrow to compete. Jesus said: *"Good measure, pressed down, shaken together, and running over."* That is the kind of blessing God is about to pour out on you. There will not be any space left for sorrow to squeeze in.

Now, let's get back to Sarah. God says,

> *"I will bless her and give you a son from her."* say it with: *"I will bring my own; I will have my own; I will have my business; I will fulfill my destiny; I will bring God the highest glory."*

Can you feel the power in those words? That is your declaration, your line in the sand against sorrow and lack.

But God is not done yet. He says, *"Now I will bless her."* And the outcome of this blessing is going to be more than just a son. God is about to compensate her for all those years of waiting; all those tears she cried in the night when she thought no one was watching.

Listen to how God emphasizes it: *"I will bless her,"* and then He adds, *"Yes, I will bless her richly."* Do you know what it means to be richly blessed? It means the blessing is so powerful, so all-encompassing that it flushes out every trace of sorrow. Remember, the Bible says the blessing of the Lord makes rich and adds no sorrow.

A blessing that does not make you rich if sorrow is still hanging around is not the full blessing God has for you. The true blessing of God comes to flush out sorrow completely, leaving your life rich in every way possible. Now, I am going to tell you something, and I want you to grab hold of it with both hands: Let it be to you according to your faith. This blessing can manifest in your health, in your body, in your mind, in your dreams, in your calling, in your future. There is not no limit to how God can bless you when you are open to receiving it.

God goes on to say about Sarah, *"Yes, I will bless her richly and make her the mother of nations. Many nations will come from her."*

This woman who couldn't have a baby, whose life was the very definition of sorrow and shame, whose efforts seemed to go unrewarded, God is promising to make her the mother of nations! Some of us do not realize that if your efforts seem to be going unrewarded, it might just be because kings are coming out of you. You are not just working for a paycheck; you are laying the foundation for a legacy that will impact nations.

Let me show you something Nehemiah 8:10 for a minute, because Nehemiah understood how to deal with sorrow. He told the people, *"Go! From today, neither be you sorry nor sorrowful. Because the joy of the Lord is your strength."* But pay attention to what characterized that joy. He did not just tell them to put on a happy face. No, he said, *"Go, eat, drink, and feast."* He was telling them, *"Go your way, eat the fat, and drink the sweets, and send portions to them for whom nothing is prepared, for this day is holy unto the Lord."* He was not telling them to go suffer or endure. He was telling them to celebrate, to enjoy the goodness of God.

If you keep your sorrow at the forefront of your mind, you are going to miss what God is doing in your life. That is why I am calling out the sorrow, so you can say goodbye to it once and for all. I want you to open your heart wide to the flood, the river of God that is coming to flush out every last bit of sorrow from your life. I do not care how many years sorrow has been camping out in your life. It is about to be flushed out. It is time for you to enjoy and celebrate the goodness of God. Nehemiah was God is representative back then, just like David was. And I am telling you here as God is representative now, declaring this word over your life.

So, when God told Abraham that Sarah would be richly blessed and give birth to kings, Abraham fell down and laughed. He could not believe what he was hearing. He said, *"God, you do not understand what you are talking about. Sarah is old. Do not worry; let Ishmael just be the baby."* He threw himself to the ground in worship, but inside, he was laughing because it did not make sense. How could all the sorrow he'd gotten used to just disappear in one year? How could God tell him that in one year, he will be lending money to banks? That in one year, he'd have his own 3,000 Airbnb properties? It seemed impossible.

Even though Abraham laughed in disbelief, he had already committed himself to God is instructions. He went ahead and circumcised himself, putting himself in a position where sorrow could be flushed out of his life. So, let me ask you: What has God been telling you? Have you been saying, *"God, I have honored you enough in this and that"*? God is asking you, *"Have you done enough? What are the instructions I have given you?"* Some of us are laughing inside, just like Abraham did, because what God is promising seems too good to be true. When Ruach Adonai, the Spirit of the Lord, shows up, He flushes out sorrow. Whatever's been stopping you from having what God said you will have, whether it is physical gold, silver, riches, or cattle, all those material things you need, God is about to break through for you.

Do not get it twisted. I know we often say material things do not hold much value, but the truth is, you need them. Look at Sarah, she had everything Abraham could give her, but the one thing she did not have was what meant more than everything to her. When Abraham tried to settle for Ishmael, saying, *"Yes, do bless Ishmael,"* God was not having it. He said, "That is not what I said. You are not smarter than me. You are not more powerful than me. Do not come and say, 'God, it is okay. I will just settle for it.' No! That is not what I said."

God is saying the same thing to you right now. You will own your castle. You will have a great family; you will have a successful life. You will not die from cancer; you will not die a loser. No sickness or disease will cut your life short. You will wake up in the morning thinking about which vehicle to drive for breakfast, whether you want to use it for meetings or lunch, or if you want to go for dinner and meet with the president. You will have vehicles; you will have yachts; you will have property; you will have material things.

Do not let your sorrow prevent this prophetic word from coming to pass. If you miss it, you might have to live through another long cycle of waiting. Remember what Nehemiah said? The blessing must be proclaimed over the people by the priests. That is what I am doing right now. I am proclaiming this blessing over you, telling you to go and enjoy the good food and sweet drinks. Give some to those who did not prepare any, because today is a special day to the Lord. Do not be sad, because the joy of the Lord will make you strong.

God is telling you, *"I want you to dare me and ask me for impossible things. If I said I am going to give you the impossible, do not try to make it easy for me. The only thing I require of you is absolute obedience."*

He is promising to keep His covenant with you forever. He is not just blessing you; He is signing a contract with you. Just like He did with Isaac before he was even born, God is ready to sign a contract with you right now.

So, here is what I want you to do: Open your heart to receive this blessing. Do not let sorrow distract you or divert your attention. Satan likes to bring sorrow to hijack your future, but I am declaring right now that every spirit of error, every Hagar in your life that is trying to sign the contract of sorrow instead of the contract of blessing, is being flushed out right now.

I am praying for the blessing of God to rest upon whoever's life has a major role in your destiny. If your Sarah is barren, let God is blessing make her fruitful. If you are the Abraham, praying for the womb of Sarah to be fertile, I am invoking this prophecy upon your head right now. God is about to bring men and women into your life who are faithful to the core, who will see your value and help you fulfill your destiny. Just like Esau begged his father for just one blessing, I am bringing this word to you from a place of deep spiritual sacrifice.

Remember, Abraham was not a bad man just because he slept with Hagar, and Sarah was not a bad woman just because she pushed

Hagar towards Abraham in a moment of desperation. They were two good people arrested by sorrow. But God is blessing was on Abraham, and now He is putting it on Sarah too. And that same blessing is coming for you. It is time to shake off the sorrow, to step into the flood of God is blessing. Your time of lack is over. Your season of abundance is here. Get ready, because God is about to do exceeding, abundantly above all you could ask or think. The sorrow's being flushed out, and the blessings rushing in. It is your time. It is your season. Receive it in Jesus' name!

CHAPTER SIX

THE ASSIGNMENT OF THE BLESSING

One of the assignments of a sorrow-free blessing is to bring increase. But not just any increase, we are talking about the kind of increase that will shock the world. This is not some minor improvement or gradual growth. No, this is an explosive, supernatural multiplication that defies human understanding and leaves people in awe. When God decides to bless you with this type of increase, it is going to be so dramatic and undeniable that even skeptics will have to sit up and take notice.

The psalmist is pouring out his heart, saying:

> *"You who have allowed me to go through all kinds of sorrow, you will not let me go down in shame. You will show up; you will revive me. Even though you have let us sink down with trials and troubles, I know you will revive us again, lifting us up from the dust, from death. Psalm 71:20-21."*

Feel the weight of David's sorrow, the desperation, but also the unshakable faith. He acknowledges that God has allowed him to experience deep sorrow and trials. He is been through the wringer and felt the crushing weight of despair. But even in that dark place, there is a flicker of hope. He knows, with absolute certainty, that God is not finished with him yet.

This verse reveals an important truth about the nature of God and His dealings with us. He does not shy away from allowing us to experience sorrow and trouble. Sometimes He even leads us into those valleys. But and this is crucial; He never abandons us there. The psalmist is confident that God will show up. Not might show up, not could show up, but will show up. And when He does, He is not coming empty-handed. He is bringing revival, restoration, and resurrection power. He is going to lift us up from the very dust of death itself.

But you cannot approach this promise of divine intervention with a casual, take-it-or-leave-it attitude. You cannot expect to experience this kind of miraculous turnaround if you are not serious about seeking God. This is not the time for half-hearted prayers or lukewarm faith. No, if you want to see God move in this extraordinary way, you need to get serious. You need to seek out someone who really knows what they are talking about, someone who has experienced the depths of sorrow and the heights of God is deliverance.

So, when you are crying out to God, begging Him to use someone to bless you, or when you sense Him calling you to be a vessel of extraordinary blessing for His people, there is a critical question you need to ask: *"Are they ready for it?"* Because let me tell you, this blessing thing we are talking about, it is not child's play. It is not some superficial, feel-good moment that fades away as soon as you leave the church building. We are talking about a blessing that has the power to completely revolutionize your life, to rewrite your story in ways you never thought possible.

One of our members was going into surgery for a procedure that was supposed to take about ten hours. It is a complex operation, that requires careful, meticulous work. But then, against all odds, she was wheeled out of the operating room after just three or four hours. Everyone's amazed, calling it a miracle. The family is praising God, the doctors are patting themselves on the back, it seems like a best-case scenario all around.

But here is where things take a dark turn. In their haste to complete the surgery quickly, the doctors missed something crucial. They touched something they shouldn't have, awakening a dormant issue that now threatens to multiply and wreak havoc on her body. What seemed like a blessing, a miraculously quick surgery has turned into a potential nightmare.

This scenario shows the delicate nature of dealing with sorrow itself. It is not something to be approached lightly or hastily. You cannot expect to address years of accumulated pain and heartache in a mere 30 minutes. Sure, you might be able to scratch the surface, to slap a Band-Aid on the wound, but you will not get to the root of the issue. And let me tell you, if you are not prepared to go deep, to really dig into the core of your sorrow, you are better off not starting the process at all. Because there is nothing more dangerous than awakening the spirit of sorrow without having the tools and the commitment to fully annihilate it from your life.

Imagine the anguish that the family will feel when they discover that the *"miracle"* they celebrated was actually a catastrophe in the making. The very thing they thought had been removed has now multiplied, spreading like wildfire through their daughter's body. The doctor cannot do anything; they have to remove this one after the other or two by two. This is a sorrow. It takes a level of sorrow dealing with somebody for your doctors to make this kind of mistake.

The only time Jesus cried in the Bible was twice tears. The first was at Lazarus' grave. The second, equally poignant, was when Jesus looked over Jerusalem, foreseeing the destruction and suffering that would befall the city. And oh, how that sorrow manifested in the years following Christ's departure from this earth. The curse that the people brought upon themselves resulted in a tragedy of epic proportions. The deaths that occurred during Jesus' time pale in comparison to the millions of Jews who perished in the wake of Hitler. This is how far-reaching the consequences of our choices and the weight of sorrow that can follow.

> *Psalm 134:1, "Come, bless the Lord, O you servants of the Lord, who by night stand in the house of the Lord. Lift up your hands and shout of victory!"*

It is clear that those who stand firm in their commitment to God, even in the darkest of nights. They are not just fair-weather believers who only show up when things are going well. No, these are the ones who remain steadfast in the house of the Lord even when the world around them is falling apart.

It is not enough to just stand there. The psalmist exhorts us to lift up our hands and shout for victory. This is not a posture of defeat or resignation. It is a bold declaration of faith, a refusal to be cowed by circumstances, a determination to praise God even when everything seems to be going wrong. This, my friends, is the secret to developing staying power in the face of adversity. The secret of my staying power is to get lost in the presence of God. To be so consumed with seeking His face that everything else fades into insignificance. Irrespective of any responsibilities I have, when the Lord says, *"I need you in My presence,"* I stay. Everything has to go on hold while I am staying and waiting. It is not always easy, mind you. There are times when the pressures of life are screaming for my attention when deadlines are looming and people are demanding my time. But I have learned that there is nothing more important than responding to that divine summons.

But when I come out of that time of waiting and seeking, every mountain has to move. There is a supernatural power that flows from those moments of intimacy with God. It is like I emerge charged with divine electricity, ready to face whatever challenges come my way. The problems that seemed insurmountable before suddenly start crumbling like sandcastles before the tide.

> Psalm 71:21: "Give us even more greatness than before, and turn and comfort us once again."

This verse is dripping with the goodness of God. It is not just about bringing us back to where we were before the trials hit. No, God is promising to elevate us to new heights of greatness, to take us further than we have ever been before. And notice the balance here along with the greatness comes comfort. It is not a cold, impersonal success, but a warm embrace of divine comfort that envelops us even as we are being promoted.

When you are comforted in this way, when you experience this divine lifting, you are given greatness greater than before, and you are given comfort forever. It is not a temporary fix or a fleeting moment of relief. This is a permanent shift in your spiritual landscape. The sorrow that once defined you becomes nothing more than a distant memory as you bask in the warmth of God is comfort and revel in the greatness, He is bestowed upon you.

Blessing In The Midst Of Emptiness

The truth about God is blessings is that they often manifest in the most unexpected times and places, particularly when we feel at our lowest or most empty.

> Haggai 2:19 (TLB): "But now, notice from today, this 15th day of the month, that the foundation of the Lord's Temple is finished, and from this day onward, I will bless you."

The Almighty is not waiting for the entire temple to be rebuilt; He is not holding out for some grand, finished product. No, He is declaring His intention to bless at the very inception, at the laying of the foundation.

It said *"Notice I am giving you this promises now, even before you have begun to rebuild the temple structure and before you have harvested your grain, and before the grapes, figs, pomegranates, and olives have produced their next crops. From this day, I will bless you."* Do you see the magnificence of what's happening here? God is not reacting to our achievements or waiting for us to prove ourselves worthy. He is proactively speaking blessing into our lives, even when there is nothing tangible to show for it yet.

He is saying, *"I want you to understand what I am doing. It is not as if you are rich and I am telling you I am going to make you rich. It is as if you have got the job, and then I am telling you I am going to give you the job. Things are working as they ought to work, and then I am telling you I will make things work."* This is a mind-bending concept, is not it? God is not just promising to enhance what we already have; He is declaring increase over what does not even exist yet in our reality.

He said, *"No, I want you to understand that I am speaking for these things now that you are nothing."* Now, do not get it twisted. This is not about God belittling us or negating our worth. On the contrary, He is emphasizing the vast chasm between our current state and the glorious future He has planned for us. It is as if He is saying, *"You are important; you are valuable. But God said you are nothing yet because God is saying you are nothing compared to what I am about to do."*

This might seem contradictory or confusing at first glance. Some of us might be in debt, some might be hanging onto a job by a thread, knowing that if we lose it, we'd be broken within months. This is not a curse. It is actually setting the stage for God is miraculous intervention. I am bringing you to a place where God is saying, *"Look at your life."* It is reminiscent of when Jesus confronted the Pharisees about their spiritual blindness. They asked Him, *"Are you trying to say we are blind?"* And Jesus, in His infinite wisdom, replied, *"You know the truth; you are blind."* Then there'd be no problem. But your problem is that you have eyes but cannot see. You are really blind, but you do not believe that you are blind.

The moment when we present our life, our case, our situation to God with complete honesty and vulnerability. It is like David's response when he received the prophecy from Nathan. He was not being negative or self-deprecating when he went to God and said, *"Who am I? What is my father's house? I am nothing. Why are You so mindful of me? Why are You speaking big about me? Who am I?"* This was an acknowledgment of his own limitations in the face of God is limitless power and love. Just like in a dream, when evil is very close, the atmosphere becomes dark and foreboding. When you wake up, the fear feels real, palpable. Similarly, when you are making certain confessions in God is presence, you need to be aware of the spiritual atmosphere. Are you speaking from a place of timidity and negativity, or from a place of humble expectation?

God knows the difference. It is entirely possible to be saying something like *"I am great"* while feeling worthless in your heart. Conversely, you might be saying, *"God, I am nothing,"* while your heart is actually declaring, *"Everything I think I am, I am nothing in comparison to what You have in store for me."* The key is alignment between your words and your heart's true belief. It is not negativity to be in God is presence with a heart of expectation, saying, *"God, you have so much in store for me, but I am looking at my life right now, and certain things are not together."* This is exactly what Hannah did. She poured out her heart, saying, *"I am not drunk; I am just a woman of a bitter soul. I have something painful; I do not have this; I want it."* And what was the response? The man of God said, *"Really? Now take it."* That is the power of honest, expectant prayer.

Now, I appreciate your spiritual maturity in recognizing that you are indeed something and somebody in God is eyes. That is crucial. But let's circle back to our scripture and really grasp what God is saying here. He is declaring, *"Now that you are nothing, now that you have nothing, I am telling you I want to make you something."* This is not about God trying to hide anything or trick us. He is being completely transparent: *"It is not as if I am telling you because you have anything that I am trying to hide under; I am telling you because I have everything that I want to give to you."*

The promise is clear and powerful: *"From this day onward, I will bless you."* God is giving us something tangible, something we can look back on and say, *"Oh, this was not here a few months ago."* And the timing of this promise is crucial; He gave it before we have even begun to rebuild the temple structure. In this context, God is saying, *"I want to begin to build or rebuild certain things in your life, and before you even start applying for any job, before you start having anything, I want you to know that I am declaring your end and I am giving you the power to get what I want you to get."*

This blessing is not contingent on our harvest or our productivity. God declares, *"And before you have harvested your grains, and before the grapes, the figs, the pomegranates, and the olives have produced their next fruits or crops, from this day, whether the enemy likes it or hates it, whether witches and wizards like it or hate it, whether curses in your family like it or hate it"* The declaration is absolute and all-encompassing: *"From this day, all these things that you were not before, I proclaimed what I proclaimed, you will become."* Whatever we had before is child's play compared to what God is about to do. *"Nothing compares to what will happen from this day; I will bless you."*

You can use this understanding to receive one blessing or a hundred blessings. From this day forward, you can start receiving everything that will cause your life to make sense. Some of these blessings you will recognize immediately, others might not be apparent at first. The key is to be quick to declare the ones you know. It is like being in an exam hall, you do not waste time agonizing over the questions you cannot answer. That is a surefire recipe for failure. Instead, you tackle the ones you know first, then come back to the more challenging ones later.

Often, the answers to the most difficult questions are hidden within the easier ones. Those seemingly insurmountable difficulties that have been breaking your head if you deal with the easy ones first, the ones you know, you will often find you have the tools to handle the tougher challenges. In your life, there are certain things that are urgent and unmistakable, like the need for housing, marriage, business opportunities, or employment. These are the *"easy questions"* you need to tackle first. Do not neglect them or put them off.

The Bible warns us about the danger of procrastination and missed opportunities: *"Say not to your neighbor, 'Go and come back tomorrow,' if you have it by you."* That spirit of non-achievement, always pushing things to *"tomorrow,"* can rob us of years of progress and blessing. It said, *"Withhold not good from him to whom it is due when it is in the power of your hand to do it; neither say to your neighbor, 'Go and come tomorrow.'"*

Think about how many people might be holding onto blessings meant for you, continually pushing you towards a *"tomorrow"* that never seems to arrive. What could have been accomplished today gets endlessly postponed. You are growing older, and yet *"tomorrow"* remains perpetually out of reach. This spirit of non-achievement, of postponed testimonies, needs to be broken in your life. For anyone who holds the key to your next phase of blessing and progress, we must pray that God preserves them. Some might argue, *"Even if they die, things will still work out."* But that is not always true. Sometimes, specific individuals play crucial roles in our destiny, and their presence or absence can significantly impact the timing and nature of our blessings.

CHAPTER SEVEN

GOD IS TIMING IN DELAYED DOORS

Pharaoh was spiritual enough to receive the dream but was not spiritual enough to know that there was someone in jail who could interpret it. He had tried all the magicians and wise people in the land, but nobody could help. It is fascinating how God works, is not it? Here we have the most powerful man in Egypt, blessed with a divine vision, yet utterly incapable of understanding its meaning. He exhausted every resource at his disposal, calling upon the brightest minds in his kingdom, only to find himself at a loss.

Then one person remembered Joseph and said, *"Ah, I remember my sin today."* God forbid if it was the case that both of them had been hanged; nobody would have remembered Joseph. Just imagine the delicate balance of God is timing here. Had events unfolded differently, had both the cupbearer and the baker met their end, Joseph's gift might have remained hidden, forgotten in the depths of that prison. It is a sobering thought, is not it? How often do we fail to recognize the intricate ways God preserves His plan, even when all seems lost?

God had to give Pharaoh a second dream so that he could understand that the answer to his first dream was in prison. That might have taken another seven years. Consider the patience of God in this moment. He did not just give Pharaoh one dream, but two, emphasizing the urgency and importance of the message. And yet, even with this double vision, Pharaoh remained blind to the solution that lay just beyond his palace walls.

If some doors had opened seven years ago, you wouldn't be where you are today. Some doors had opened seven years ago, but guess what? God said, *"From today, I am changing things."* Think for a moment. How many times have we lamented over opportunities missed, doors that remained stubbornly closed despite our best efforts? Yet here is a truth: those very delays, frustrating as they may have been, were instrumental in shaping our present reality. And now, at this precise moment, God declares a shift, a divine turning point that promises to alter the course of our journey.

So, what I told God is, *"Lord, whatever I am, whatever I have, I am nothing."* You and I now, right now, where I am, this is my ground zero. It is not negative, Lord; this is my ground zero. Let's start from here. This declaration is not one of self-deprecation, but of radical humility and surrender. By acknowledging our complete dependence on God, we position ourselves for His intervention. Ground zero, it is a powerful concept, is not it? It speaks of new beginnings, of limitless potential, of a fresh canvas upon which God can paint His masterpiece.

Imagine if everybody has my present as their ground zero; that is a good ground zero. So, if after 25 or 27 years of working with the Lord, this is how far He has brought me, and I am saying, *"Lord, this is ground zero; I have not started. I want to start today because You told me that from today You will bless me."* He said, *"Okay, let's start."*

So, imagine what will happen in the next 365 days of my life. Bless Him! Favor, favor everywhere! God did it, and everyone sees it.

I think this prayer came to my spirit, and I mentioned it to you: I pray that the person who is the key master key to your next glory will not lose favor with you, that they will not look at you and find something that irritates them. Sometimes, our breakthrough is connected to specific individuals, gatekeepers, if you will, whom God has positioned to play a crucial role in our elevation.

The blessing of God makes rich and adds no sorrow. I have just removed a major sorrow from your life. One of the evidences of God is blessing is that when God blesses you, He gives you compassion in the sight of the key to your next level. The same way you are also a key to someone else's next level. The brothers of Joseph had compassion in the sight of Joseph. He could have killed them, but he wept; he did not kill them. He received them, blessed them, and protected them. This profound insight illuminates the cyclical nature of God is blessing. When we are favored, it often manifests as undeserved grace from others. Simultaneously, we become vessels of that same grace towards those in our sphere of influence.

When you lose compassion in the sight of the one God meant to take you to the next level, your life becomes very complicated. Another prayer I am praying for you is this: Any man, any woman, any mortal, please understand that God does not want to depend on any man. But the way God works is that He works through men, through people. Every individual who is supposed to play a vital role in the practical manifestation or materialization of your blessing whether man or woman, wherever they are will not die before your presence manifests. The men and women that are your destiny gatekeepers may God keep them for you.

One lady did not know that the spirit of death was hunting her husband. She started dreaming even before she got married. In her dreams, she would see that she was with a man, and all of a sudden, he would leave the car or disappear. Sometimes something would happen, sometimes it would not; maybe they went to the beach, and something just took him away.

So, when she met the guy, she was going to marry, she did not take her time to study things about him. She thought that maybe the guy was going to break her heart, not knowing that it was the spirit of death hunting him to kill any man she would marry. Eventually, she married this guy, a very nice guy, a godly man. But they did not go through deliverance; they did not break any curses. They were overly excited with love and got married. Everything went well and was sweet and smooth until one week later, when the guy was dead.

Do not be scared; listen. God will not bring a story that is not meant to fix somebody's mockery and change somebody's story. In your case, it may not be a man or woman; in your case, it might be that one boss who is meant to teach you the business or the field that God has called you to master. Just because it is time for God to use them to teach you things, the enemy shows up and attacks, unfortunately killing the person, because Satan knows he cannot kill you.

So, if he cannot kill you, he looks for anything that will limit your life, that will stop you. And that is why we are dealing with the blessing, the eliminator of sorrow. I want you to pray this prays as we end this section;

I will never lose favor with any man any woman and everyone whose life, presence, influence, or position has something good to do with my destiny. I will never lose favor; my destiny connector will never get to a point where they feel irritated and they will not give up on me.

The Danger Of Wrong Associations

In the journey of life, we are surrounded by various individuals, each playing a unique role in shaping our destinies. However, not all associations are beneficial, and some can even pose significant dangers to our spiritual and personal growth. Let me show you something about the life of David.

2 Samuel 21:17

"They told David, 'You shall no longer go out to fight, lest

you quench the lamp of Israel.'"

Here we see David, the warrior king, being advised by his subjects to refrain from personally engaging in battle. There are people who are delighting lights in our lives. Whether you like it or not, there are battles you can fight because you do not have enough eyes to see, and even those who have eyes to see may not have the strategies to fight. They said to David, *"You shall no longer go out with us to battle, lest you quench the lamp of Israel."* David is likened to a lamp, a source of light and guidance for the entire nation. His life, his leadership, and his very presence among the people were deemed so crucial that the risk of losing him in battle was considered too great to bear. This speaks volumes about the impact that key individuals can have in our lives.

In your life, who are the *"lamps"* that God has placed around you? These are the individuals who bring light to your paths, who illuminate the way forward when you are in dark and uncertain times. They could be spiritual mentors, wise counselors, or even family members whose godly influence shapes our decisions and character. Just as David was.

Any man, any woman that is a light, that is brightness in your life, may God cause them to live long. I came across a photograph of my spiritual father standing alongside a woman, and in that moment, my spirit was stirred to intercession. Without hesitation, I lifted my voice to God, pleading, *"Cause them to live long."* You see, these individuals are more than just casual acquaintances or even respected figures, they are path lights in my life. Their influence extends beyond mere words or actions; their very existence serves as a source of guidance and inspiration.

There are times when I find myself grappling with questions, uncertainties that seem to cloud my judgment. In those moments, I do not even need to pick up the phone or send a message. Simply gazing upon their pictures often provides the clarity and answers I seek. It is as if their lives serve as a living testament to God is wisdom and grace, offering silent counsel even in their absence.

This realization compels me to pray fervently for them: *"Let them live long; let their children prosper; let sorrow be far from them; let them be filled with joy as they serve."* These are not mere platitudes or casual wishes; they are heartfelt petitions born out of a deep appreciation for the role these *"lamps"* play in my life. You must recognize your Spiritual well-being and continued influence are intricately tied to your spiritual growth and effectiveness in God is kingdom.

However, as we are looking at the blessings of the right associations, you must also confront the fact that not all connections in your life are beneficial. There may be individuals in your immediate circle who, unbeknownst to you, carry a death sentence not in the literal sense, but in terms of their spiritual influence. Their presence in your life may be slowly extinguishing your light, dampening your fervor for God, or leading you astray from your divine purpose.

Any death sentence hanging over those who are meant to be lights in my life, I cancel it in Jesus' name! For others, the situation may be different. Perhaps there are people who have invested heavily in your life, mentors, teachers, parents, or friends who have poured their time, resources, and wisdom into your development. Yet, for various reasons, they have not seen the fruits of their labor. From their perspective, it might appear as though their investment in you has been in vain. To such individuals, I declare this powerful truth: they will not depart from this earth until they witness the undeniable evidence that their investment in you was not wasted. God, in His faithfulness, will ensure that they see the harvest of seeds they have sown into your life.

I was ministering to my pastors and told them about a vision I saw about excitement. I said, *"This is something you must cherish: God gives you an indescribable excitement; that is a gift."* The significance of this divine gift cannot be overstated, especially in light of the spiritual battles we face daily.

Why does God bestow upon us this gift of indescribable excitement? More often than not, it serves as a powerful antidote to the spirit of depression that frequently hovers around us, seeking to rob us of our joy and vitality in Christ. This divine excitement is a shield, that will prevent you from succumbing to despair. It is a tangible manifestation of God is grace, that will empower you to maintain a positive outlook even in the face of challenging situations.

Let me be clear on this point: the primary catalyst for depression is distance from God. Many may resist this truth, preferring to attribute their emotional state to external circumstances or biological factors. While these can certainly play a role, we must not overlook the spiritual dimension. I assert with conviction that any person who remains in a state of depression for an extended period, be it an hour or two, in that moment, drifted far from the presence of God.

We must guard against the deception that such emotional turmoil is simply an inevitable part of life. No, that is not the abundant life Jesus promised when He declared,

> *"I have come that they may have life, and have it more abundantly" (John 10:10).*

We have the power to choose the life we live; we can either settle for the life we naturally have or embrace the abundant life Christ offers.

One of the most compelling evidence of closeness to God is what the apostle Peter describes as *"joy unspeakable and full of glory"* (1 Peter 1:8). This supernatural joy serves as a bulwark against the attacks of depression. When those dark thoughts attempt to assail your mind, they should not find a foothold for more than a few moments. Even ten minutes is too long to entertain such negativity; two minutes should be sufficient time to recognize the attack and rebuke it. We must learn to forcefully command these depressive thoughts to depart from our mental and emotional space.

How can you discern whether you have strayed from intimate communion with God? One clear indicator is your response to trials and tribulations. When you find yourself unable to *"count it all joy when you fall into various trials,"* as James 1:2 exhorts us to do, it is a sign that your spiritual alignment may be off. Conversely, a heart that is closely attuned to God is presence can maintain a joyful countenance even in the midst of hellish circumstances.

I told my pastors, *"I see what people do not see and know what people do not know. Take my prayers seriously. Even if you do not fully comprehend them in the moment, heed them with reverence."* I emphasized that while I may not always provide an immediate explanation for every prayer, the act of faithfully praying as directed can catalyze life-altering transformations. I instructed them to apply these prayers not only to their personal lives but also to their families and congregations. One specific directive I gave was to aggressively confront any suicidal spirits lurking in their midst. *"Chase them out,"* I urged. *"Let the presence of Christ drive them far away."* This is not mere rhetoric; it is a call to spiritual warfare, recognizing the very real dangers that can manifest when we neglect to maintain vigilance over our spiritual atmosphere.

You see, without spiritual sensitivity, it is all too easy to overlook or dismiss seemingly insignificant signs that may actually be harbingers of serious spiritual attacks. That is why I gathered my pastors, imparting these crucial insights and leading them in fervent prayer.

We were having a rehearsal some time ago for my song *"Open the Eyes of Men."* One of the pastors had to step out to take a distressing call from his wife. When he returned, he was visibly shaken, I inquired about the situation. He revealed that his wife was hearing a voice urging her to *"end it all"* in other words, to take her own life. This was not a woman living in abject circumstances;

on the contrary, she enjoyed a life that many would envy, blessed with a loving family and material comfort. Yet, here she was, grappling with thoughts of suicide.

When I bring something like this, take it seriously. No matter the price you have to pay in terms of time. Unfortunately, some believers tend to treat prophetic utterances with a degree of nonchalance, perhaps because they are not being charged a fee for the insight. But I implore you: do not wait until you become a victim of the very things you neglected to address when you had the opportunity. The price of spiritual negligence is far too high.

I pronounce this powerful declaration over your life: May you become a source of irritation to evil and wicked individuals, those who have no rightful place in your life or destiny. Let their discomfort in your presence serve as a divine strategy to remove them from your sphere of influence. Remember, even a single day spent in the company of the wrong person can have far-reaching, negative consequences. When such individuals appear in your life, God often provides clear signals and warnings. The question is: Are we attuned enough to His voice to heed these warnings?

I fervently pray that, by God is mercy, He will actively irritate and displace every wrong association in your life. And when this divine irritation takes effect, causing these detrimental influences to depart, may you possess the wisdom and discernment not to foolishly attempt to reconcile with them. Do not fall into the trap of apologizing or trying to smooth things over when God is orchestrating their removal for your protection and advancement.

Protecting The Blessings

Haggai 2:19: "So God said, from this day I will bless....."

To bless means to be empowered, to succeed, to be given the ability both the cognitive ability, the inner ability, and the destiny ability to succeed against all odds. But the blessing is not just so you succeed against all odds; it is the eliminator of sorrow.

I showed you earlier how every time there is a blessing, where you find sugar, you find ants; where you see light, you find insects. Everywhere there is a blessing, it is magnetic. A blessing is meant to make things beautiful. Satan is drawn to beautiful things, not because he likes them, but because he is the king of destruction. He hates beautiful things.

That is why, when my kids were growing up, one of the things we did not do was prevent them from running around and scattering things. When they wanted to move around and scatter things, my wife said, *"Oh no!"* I said, *"Leave them."* So instead of stopping them, I said, *"Hey, come here, look."* We taught them things so they learned early on, and we did not have to deal with children breaking this or that. You know that saying *"Every child will break something."* My kids did not break anything.

Their worst funny thing; I do not want to say they spoiled something, but they did manage to get slime on the carpet yes, in their room, until they managed to take it to our room. But to say they broke something, they did not. Why? Whenever they wanted to spoil something, the normal thing for a parent is to shout, *"No! Stop it!"* All of you parents are making choices to stop something. You instigate their curiosity, and sometimes there is that thing that talks to that child; they want to see what you will do.

Whether you like it or not, you are not the first parent; this is just children. If you have not read about parenting, you are robbing yourself and hurting your children. Some people have children, yet they know nothing about raising kids. You do not know the psychological aspects; you do not know the spiritual aspects. Yet, there are books. My spiritual grandmother (Mama Oyedepo) has written books, Bishop David Ibiyeomie's wife has written books. There are many books on raising godly children, yet some Christian mothers have not even read one. So, they raise their children based on their child's reaction, not knowing that every action of a child is a prophecy of what will happen in the next year, month, or few months ahead. You have to be intentional.

So, when your kids are trying to spoil something. Don not be in haste to want to stop the. God gave them brains; they are not going to spoil things, but there is something within them that is curious and wants to explore. For those of you that do not have kids yet, start reading about kids. Some of you are experts in your place of work but know nothing about raising children. You have read all the research in the world and can tell everything better than even Dr. Fauci.

You have to learn about raising children. You know everything about your job, don not you? If you are a parent, your number one job is raising godly children, raising children God will be proud of. I was talking to one of my little boys here sometimes; he came to my office, and then he had his hair braided. I told him I do not like braids. He said, *"Oh, yeah, I like braids."* I said, *"I do not like braids."* I said, *"You, as a man, why like braids? I said I prefer dreads for a man."* He said, *"Why?"* I said, *"You are a man; do not use braids to look like a woman. You should be a man."* When you see those stupid Cecil things showing up in children, Cecil demons on them, cast them out of the children because they are pushing it in school, and some of their teachers are possessed with demons. So, you must be intentional. When you see a boy, tell him, *"Be a man. Come on, do not cry; be a man."* Well, they say, *"Oh, stop telling men to be a man."* Does that mean men do not cry? Men do not cry, at least we do not let you see our cry. If your wife is crying and you are crying, you are a Cecil; you are a child. If you want to cry, look for another man who is a man and cry before him, wipe your tears, and go back. That is how leaders do.

Now, they have turned men into vegetables, and now they are turning women into something else. I told the young boy, I said, *"Dude, I do not like braids because it makes you look like a woman. Be a man."* The boy standing there might probably not be more than 10 years old. But he asked me a question: *"But I thought that God gave us the will to choose what we want to do today?"* A small boy not more than 10 said, *"Did not God give us the will to do what we want to do with our lives and our bodies?"* I said, *"Yes."*

Then, I was eating, so I picked up the knife, grabbed his hand, and he started shaking, and vibrating. Now, you do not threaten kids with a knife, okay? Do not do that. But he was vibrating. I said, *"Right now, I have the will to stab you with this knife; it is my God-given will, so can I use it?"* He said, *"No."* I said, *"So you see if everybody used their free will to do what they feel like doing, right now what I feel like doing is to stab you. I asked him, 'Am I using my will, right?'* He said, *'No.'* I said, *'That is it,' and then I pulled the knife because I did not want the knife to be his last experience."*

Then I now said, *"Okay, now what if I feel like I want to hit you, and it is my free will; does that mean I am using my free will right?"* He said, *"No."* He got that message now. He said people are bullying him in school. I said, "That is why you need to be a man. Get rid of those braids; keep dreads. If you carry braids, they think you are a chicken not that women are chickens but if you see a female carry braids, that is a blessing, right? And carrying dreads is also okay. When you see a woman carry braids, it is a blessing; they look nice and beautiful and they are feminine braids or hair or any of those nice things.

But when a man is wearing braids, I do not care if he is a superstar or whoever; if your role model is a hair breeder, there is a Cecil spirit in him. Go and tell him to get rid of the braids. I said so. Until somebody begins to speak sense into reality, that is how we just sit and watch everybody do stupid things and have a society where you do not have strong men, bold men; you have chicken-hearted men. And then you see the women now trying to be men, and later the men have lost their ability to be men, so now they want to intimidate women by now trying to say they are females.

So now the men are trying to be women. I do not care if you go and implant breasts; you cannot have a menstrual cycle. You do not know what it means to have menstruation, and that is the point.

All of you women, you are letting this chicken man, who does not know how to face the reality of masculinity, try to turn your femininity into something else. No, all of you women, you are going to rise; you will succeed as women, and you will be proud to be women, and you will not call any stupid man who wants to be a woman *"her."*

I believe that the Holy Spirit wants me to throw this out. It may not be for you now. It might be for somebody who will read it later or hear it through your mouth and get angry and mad at me. But two weeks later, there will say, *"This guy is making sense."* Even the most perverse will know I am making sense. It is time for men to be men and women to be women. Women enjoy being women; let's enjoy looking at their beauty and their shapes and all the blessings God gave them. Not that one man will go to the gym and work and have six packs, then come and dress and say, *"I am a female,"* then he is making the woman that has no pack feel like she is nothing. That said, make sure you learn how to raise your children. Go and learn.

So do not push your kids away from God is purpose for them. This, to us, is how to remove sorrow, okay? So do not pull your kids away into curiosity; teach them how to handle it. I know you can snatch the knife so they do not cut themselves, but what's the benefit of snatching the knife and dropping it and getting mad? Tomorrow, there will look for that knife and still repeat the intention in their hearts.

Satan likes beautiful things, not because it is attracted to beautiful things, but as a destroyer of beautiful things. So, when you are being blessed, you must make sure your blessing is protected without sorrow. He brings sorrow, but yours will have no sorrow. You have your children trying to put something at home; hold their hands. I said, *"Oh, it is okay, come help me do it; let's fix it." You will be so shocked at how intelligent your kids are. The next time they want to destroy it, you say, "Excuse me, you just fixed this thing; are you going to spoil what you fixed?" "Oh, no!"*

Now, even if they scatter what they fixed, bring them back to fix it. After a little bit, after a while, they will now learn, and they will change. Believe you me, this is a 33.3 million dollars counsel I gave you. Take it; you might think that you do not need it now, but later, you are going to thank me. So, I want you to ask God for a manifested blessing. You will use your words to say, *"God, you said from this thing You will bless me."*

If you look at Deuteronomy, all those curses God said He would put on people who disobey Him, flip them, and you will find out that all of them are blessings, but they are short, while the curse is everlasting. Instead of fever, sound health; instead of boils, sound health; instead of cancer, sound health. He said, *"I will make sure that instead of you serving your enemies, let your enemies serve you."* When Noah cursed Ham, he said, *"Because of you, Canaan shall be a servant of servants."* Can you imagine? He blessed Japheth and cursed Canaan, saying Canaan would be a slave to Japheth. So, the people that are blessed cannot be enslaved, but the people that are blessed will have slaves. Now, I am not saying you should go and buy slaves; that is not what I mean. I am not promoting slavery.

I am saying life cannot enslave you if you are blessed. If you are blessed, now that you are asking God, nobody can come and tell you that you are cursed, and any curse that is expressing itself in your life through sorrow is wiped out completely. So, I want you to take your business. I believe with all my heart that since the devil is a destroyer, God said, *"From today, I will bless you."* God has beautified your lives; nothing can bring ugliness and sorrow into your life.

CHAPTER EIGHT

GARMENTS AND SHAPES SORROW COMES IN

You see, the adversary, that old serpent called the devil, doth not approach us with boldness, lest all might perceive his true nature. Nay, in the garden, he slithered forth as a cunning serpent, beguiling Eve with poisonous words. Throughout the ages, this deceiver did not stop disguising himself seeking to pilfer the blessings bestowed upon us by the Almighty.

As I have said earlier, the enemy is drawn to that which gleams with beauty and radiance. His covetous gaze is fixed upon every blessing, everything good and pure that God has given us. Thus, it behooves us to comprehend the wiles and stratagems of this foe, that we might stand firm against his assaults.

He employed cunning disguises and deceitful words to lead us astray. He cometh not as just a roaring lion. No. But as an angel of light, his darkness cloaked in a garment of false righteousness. Yea, he seeketh to infiltrate our minds with thoughts of sorrow, and unbelief, that he might steal, kill, and destroy. But the mark of God as exempted you from this wickedness in Jesus' name.

Sorrow Comes Packaged In Foes Pretending To Be Friends

Proverbs 10:18-23 (TPT): The one who hides hatred while pretending to be your friend is nothing but a liar.

Trust is the hardest currency in this life. It is very hard to earn, but when a person trusts an individual, they start opening up and sharing their personal issues and secrets. You may not know when you are confiding in a foe, thinking that foe is a friend.

Because most often than not, foes have very tactical ways of hiding their hatred for you. Hatred does not mean, *"I hate you; I want to kill you."* Hatred can manifest in many forms, such as desiring your life while simultaneously resenting you for it. They may say, *"Your life is the life I wish I could have, but since I cannot have it, I hate you."*

The thing about haters is they do not realize that even the best lives have their own issues. Life has issues; everybody has one, two, three, or even five issues they are dealing with. There is no human on this earth who does not have a secret. Everybody has secrets, and everybody tends to want to trust someone with their secrets. I have found in this life that the number one person to trust with your secret is yourself. Then, maybe the second person to trust with your secrets is someone who already knows them.

You know what makes my life easy? I am the number one gossip about my life. Oh yes, that is how I defeated all my enemies! When they gossip about me, I climb the pulpit and gossip about myself. So, what are you trying to say about me that I have not already said? I say it from the pulpit, and it dies.

I told the pastors some time ago about someone I used to like and admire, but there are just some things I do not like about him at all. No matter how I feel about him, there is one thing I can say:

the guy just refuses to die. This guy's name is spared; he is here in America. His wife was pregnant, and he impregnated a young girl and her mother. They all gave birth to their children in the same month. The girlfriend gave birth to twins, and her mother gave birth to one.

Everybody said it was over for him, even those with issues and unclean spirits following them. They said it was over for him. His own spiritual father said it was over for him. One of his spiritual brothers said, *"That is it."* This guy is moving from one state to another. I am not saying whatever he did is good, but for whatever reason, he refuses to be canceled.

Instead of standing against the counselors, he joined the counselors. So, he joined those parties and those people who are the ones counseling others. You know, the moment they feel like you are with them, they do not counsel you. The only time they counsel you is when you start working against them. Then there will dig up all your secrets and say, *"Bring me everything you know about him,"* and they will put it out there.

So now, the thing is that this individual is still doing what he is doing. That alone is strength, either demonic or divine. But here is the point I am trying to make: if you trust the wrong person, weak people are kings and queens of blackmail. And blackmail does not just mean that someone comes and says, *"Hey, this is what I know about you; pay me this amount of money, and I will not say it."*

One thing you must know is that if you pay a blackmailer one penny, you will be paying them until you die. When people think they know something about you, weak, useless people will use it against you, and sometimes it causes sorrow.

Ahithophel was a trusted friend of David, but he could not hide his hatred for David. He was David's counselor, but his eyes were on the throne, so he looked for every way to eliminate David. David went back to the One who blessed him.

David prayed to God because Ahithophel gave David's son the most perfect counsel to destroy David. Now, Ahithophel knew that even though Absalom might succeed in destroying David by following that counsel, David's men would still kill Absalom. So, who would be the next person in power? Ahithophel.

There are times when your life is easier and better when you know this enemy is an enemy. People say, *"If you are going to die with the devil, use a long spoon."* Why must you die with the devil in the first place? Why must it get access to your dining table?

In this life, people who are foes pretending to be friends can bring you sorrow. But what is the blessing? It is divine empowerment to succeed against all odds, against adversaries, against satanic traps not just against adversaries but against adversities. The blessing is direct access to the protection and preservation of God.

The Power Of Divine Protection

So, when human beings hide their hatred for you while pretending to be your friends those are liars and foes pretending to be friends around you suddenly, they may find ways to hurt you or use your children against you, attacking all kinds of things.

When it seems like they are almost winning, David turned to the blesser and said, *"O God, turn the counsel of Ahithophel into foolishness."* You may think that was just a simple prayer, but not when a blessed man, anointed by God, prays such prayers. That was a suicidal missile released by the blessed one! God said, *"I will curse anyone that curses you. Anyone that gives counsel against you, anyone that conspires against you, shall surely gather, but not by Me. Whoever gathers together against you shall fall for your sake."*

So, what did David do? David sentenced Ahithophel to death. You cannot tell me that just because your counsel was rejected, you would go and die unless the voice of the blessed person is haunting you, it will make you take your own weapon. That is what the Bible says in Psalms 35:13: *"Let their own sword pierce their hearts."*

Listen to me: if your determination is to rise by the blessing, then you must eliminate every sorrow. Sorrows hide or come when foes are pretending to be friends. He says, *"Let his own sword pierce unto his own heart."*

> In Psalm 37:13,15-17(MSG): *"The Lord is laughing at those who plot against the godly, for He knows their judgment is near. Evil men take aim to slay the poor, the righteous, the godly, and the good men. They are ready to butcher those who do right.... But their sword will be plunged into their own heart, and all their weapons will be broken. It is better to have little and be godly than to own an evil man's wealth, for evil people want to become wealthy off of the good. For the strength of evil men shall be broken, but the Lord takes care of those He has forgiven."*

While people look at you and perhaps you made a mistake or missed the mark, they wait for your weak moment to strike at you. God says, *"Do not worry; the number one thing you need is the blessing of forgiveness."*

The Bible says, *"Blessed is the man whose sin is forgiven".* There is a blessing upon the blessed when your sins are forgiven. But when evil men do not consider their wickedness, they are going about trying to destroy you, or foes are close to you trying to take things about you or look for your secrets, they are on a path to suicide.

For the Lord gets off all His forgiven ones, while the strength of the evil will surely disappear. David said, *"God, let the counsel of Ahithophel be turned into foolishness."* That means put a hit on Ahithophel, who pretended to be my son's friend. Put him in a place where he will kill himself.

God told Abimelech one day because Abimelech thought he was right. He said, *"Abraham is a prophet; return what you took from him, otherwise I will keep you and kill your household, I will kill your nation. Return everything."* Let me tell you: the power of the blessing will annihilate sorrow.

Sorrow comes dressed like a friend. Should you not have friends? You ought to have friends. So, should you not trust someone? Yes, begin with trusting in the Lord and trusting in yourself. Let your secret be your secret.

If there is someone you think can keep a secret, then you can share, but I do not think there are some things I know that until I meet with Jesus, no human being on earth will know. I do not care who you are; you can be anything to me, but you still will not know.

Even the Almighty God is God because He is a possessor of secrets. The Bible says the secret things belong to God; the things revealed are for us. If you really want to know my secret, go in the spirit. And if your eyes go blind forever, blame yourself.

Yeah, you want to search me in the spirit? Go ahead! You are a prophet, you are a prophetess, you are a preacher, you are a prayer warrior. Go and look for me in the spirit. When you see what I represent in the spirit, you will come and give me a sacrifice; you will come and give me an offering.

Job was going through all kinds of trials, and his friends came pretending to be real friends. But when God exposed them, they were shocked. God said, *"All of you go to Job."* Job was to pray for them. God warned them, *"You are about to die; I will kill all of you."* He said, *"Take an offering not to give to Me, but to give to Job."*

What happened to Job? How did he reach that level? He was a blessed man. He was so blessed that even Satan confirmed that God had blessed everything Job had. Satan couldn't penetrate Job, so when challenges came, he used his friends to frustrate him, foes pretending to be friends.

Wisdom In Navigating Relationships

Some people ask, *"Can you trust again?"* Yes, but be wise. When you see the principles of how to forgive and take their sins off your record, you will be able to say to yourself, *"It is worth it to help a friend; it is worth it to love."* But you must also be wise because not everyone will understand. That said.

> *In Job 42:7 (LBT), it says, "After the Lord had finished speaking with Job, he said to Eliphaz the Temanite, 'I am angry with you and your two friends, for you have not been right in what you have said about me, as my servant Job has.'"*

Now take seven young bulls. God showed them how to escape. He said, *"Take an offering."* I am literally saying this: there are some people to whom you need to take seven bulls. This is your solution; otherwise, you will continue to struggle.

There is someone I know who has had three failed marriages. He married a Nigerian, and the marriage failed. Then he married an American, and that marriage failed too. He then married a Zimbabwean, and that marriage also failed. Now, maybe he will marry an alien because he is on the path to multiple failures. Do not laugh at a person when you do not know; you have not faced your own battles. Do not laugh when you have not explored certain fields.

It was the same Samuel, a boy God raised to replace Eli's sons, that when he became the great man of God, his own sons became the exact thing that Eli's sons were sons of Belial.

So, God instructed, *"Now take seven young bulls and seven rams and go to my servant Job and offer a burnt offering for yourselves."* Job was a spiritual entity that these guys did not understand. His life was so significant that the demons could not attack him.

He took on Satan himself; the first attack failed, and when the second attack came, it also failed. The friends of Job did not realize that he was going through a major trial almost like being a victim of God is argument with Satan.

You know, there is an African proverb that says, *"When two elephants fight in the bush, it is the trees and the grass that suffer the consequences."* When an elephant is angry, instead of attacking another elephant, it attacks the trees. The trees and grass become the victims.

These men did not know that Job was a major force to be reckoned with in the spiritual realm; his current situation was a result of a divine debate between God and Satan. So, when people do not know you, it is important for you to know yourself. Know your walk with God. Know that you are saved, sanctified, and a child of God. Know that your sins are forgiven and that you are filled with the Holy Spirit. Know that you are seated together with Christ in heavenly places.

The Bible says, *"And we know that we are of God and have overcome the world, for greater is He that is in us than he that is in the world."* Know yourself! Know who you are in Christ! Understand that you are blessed beyond curses. Know that the blessing of Abraham has paralyzed any curse hanging over you, and when you connect by faith through the help of the Holy Spirit, you become a partaker of that blessing.

God said, *"Take the sacrifice for yourselves, and my servant Job will pray for you, and I will accept his prayer on your behalf."* I pray for you: may the blessings of God come upon you. Amen! I command the blessings of God to rest upon you. May God accept my prayer on your behalf. May the mercies of God envelope you. May the grace of God help me love you in the name of Jesus.

And God will not destroy you as I should because of your sin. What was their sin? It was their failure to speak rightly concerning Job. You do not know what some people represent in the spirit realm. I was told of a woman who went to the hospital a month ago. Her daughter had just gotten married, and everything seemed to be going well. She was a powerful woman who went to the hospital because she was feeling a little strange. After running some tests, the doctor found that she had stage 4 breast cancer. The doctor said, *"There is nothing we can do."*

So, the daughter left me a message crying, saying, *"The doctor said there is nothing we can do; it is stage 4 cancer."* Let me tell you, child of God, Satan wants to bring sorrow. How can it be that your daughter just got married, and you have not even seen the baby yet, but now you have stage 4 cancer? God said, *"I will not destroy you as I should because of your sin, your failure to speak rightly concerning my servant Job."* They spoke according to what they saw; they spoke according to what their senses knew. So, they said all manner of things against Job, thinking they were right. They told Job to shut up, claiming he must have iniquity in his house. They made Job start swearing, which he had never done before. And God got angry; that is when God began to speak.

Job had to swear to convince them. Do not ever make a good man swear to convince you. If they want to swear, run away! It is very destructive. Job said to them, *"Oh, I swear to you, if I have ever done this or that..."*

Let me tell you: most times, people make certain mistakes, and God gives room to change. So, God said to them, *"Take an offering to Job."* He warned them that if they did not, He would destroy them because they did not speak well of Job. Who was Job? He was like their friend, but they did not realize that Job was also a deity.

Before COVID-19, God revealed to me that something terrible was coming. He instructed us to fast. Thank God for the church and its amazing people; they obeyed, and we fasted on Thanksgiving Day. God shows me scary things because there are dead prophets in our days who have become so weak that people have turned them into vegetables. If God shows them something dark, they will fight the prophet. Not me! That is why I do not charge for prophecy, and I do not beg anybody for a favor. I serve people out of love and genuineness.

You cannot throw fresh fish under your carpet and then wonder why your house smells a few days later. Have you ever put meat or fish in your car, and the blood-stained it? It does not leave the car. In winter, it stinks; in summer, it perfumes. Blood is so dangerous! That is why, when David said he wanted to drink water from the wells of Bethlehem, his soldiers went and brought the water. He said, *"What? This is not water; this is the blood of men."* He did not drink it; he poured it out before God.

So, people like us, some of you are drinking our blood. Most of you do not know you have been drinking my blood because you do not know how many hours, I sleep to be able to serve you. Even the few hours I manage to sleep, I am still seeing visions. It seems like when my humanity is trying to rest, my divinity is traveling everywhere. Thank God gives His beloved sleep!

I am not saying this for my sake, but because many of you, by virtue of God is work in you, are becoming deities. We cannot take over this world as humans. Moses tried to deliver Israel as a human, and he was the one who ran away when God visited him. The scripture says God started walking, and when God walked, what did He do? He told Moses, *"See, I have made you a god to Pharaoh"* (Exodus 7:1). He said, *"Go; your brother will be your prophet."* So, you are the god telling your brother what to prophesy.

I am telling you, the prophecy I am giving you here is yours to take. Feel free to go and prophesy! *"I have made you a god."* We cannot take this nation or deliver it as humans. All the people working for Satan have changed their status; they are now highly demonic. So, God is not looking for humans to deliver humans. He is looking for human gods. *"I have said, 'Ye are gods'"* (Psalm 82:6). Imagine if a god comes here to deliver the nation, and a human decides, *"I am going to kill a god."*

He showed us in the Book of Revelation about the two witnesses. He said, *"When they come and begin to manifest, they have the power to call down fire from heaven; they can open and close the heavens. No one can kill them. Anyone who tries to kill them will die."* Until a day will come when they will be killed, and then they will resurrect again after three days.

So, God said, *"Go, because of what you said against my servant Job; make a sacrifice."* The Bible makes it clear that you can have pretenders, foes pretending to be friends. It is better not to be someone's friend than to be a foe pretending to be a friend.

"The measure with which you measure for others will be the same that will be used in measuring for you," except that yours will now be multiplied a thousandfold. That is why gossips do not carry anointing; they do not go far with God. They always hit rock bottom. Whether you are male or female, if your mouth leaks like a chicken behind, you cannot go far. Some people have mouth diarrhea; they cannot keep quiet. They feel obligated to talk, so when there is nothing to say, they formulate something to say. When they begin to say what should not be said, they end up lying.

So, what happened? The Bible says, *"Their own sword will pierce through their heart."* Ahithophel, who brought sorrow to David, ended up dying because the blessing of God annihilates sorrow. When humans decide to be your source of sorrow, if you are the blessed one, guess what will happen? That soul will be annihilated.

Learning From Abigail's Experience

I remember a good story: the story of Nabal. David had helped him with everything, and his men had assisted him in his endeavors. David sent his men to request something from Nabal. When those men approached, Nabal insulted them, saying, *"Depart from my presence! Go and tell David, 'You who are running away from your boss, you rebel!'"* David was angry and gathered his men, ready to kill Nabal.

Guess what? Nabal's wife, Abigail, came out with all manner of offerings. She said to David, *"Please receive this blessing from my hand."* Abigail told David, *"Do not you know that this man, Nabal, is a fool? His name means 'fool,' and he is a fool. Please receive, I pray thee, this blessing from my hand. I forgive him."*

David replied, *"May God bless you, wise woman, for being so discerning. I swear, if not for you, I would have killed this man."* David said, *"Blessed be the Lord God of Israel, who sent you to meet me today."*

So, what happened? That night, Nabal went to bed and did not wake up. It was David who protected Nabal's cattle; even Nabal's men said, *"This is the man who fights for us. He never stole from us; he never took anything."* Soon after David learned that Nabal had died, he said, *"I need that wise woman on my team. Bring me that Abigail."* He said, *"Please, Abigail, come and be my wife."*

"She arose, bowed herself on her face to the earth, and said, 'Behold, thy handmaid! Let thy handmaid be a servant to wash the feet of the servants of my Lord.'"

Big mistake! You wash the feet of your Lord, not of His servants. Do not ever make your Lord feel like there is competition or that any of His servants are as important as you are. Even when I am talking to important people, when my father calls me or shows up, I drop their call. I do not look at my father's call and say, *"Oh, I will call him back."* Even when I am on the pulpit, sometimes I have to say, *"Please, somebody can do that,"* and he knows that I do not want to wash the feet of my Lord's servants.

But the fact that she eventually became his wife was already a blessing. The foolish guy, Nabal, died, and Abigail became David's wife. Abigail, who had wisdom and was supposed to be a powerful woman in David's life, forgot herself and failed to develop herself to meet his royal status. She married him when he was still a hoodlum, jumping around and killing people. She traveled with him, facing all the challenges, but now this man had become a king. She was still thinking like a gangster, not realizing that he no longer needed to steal from anyone; whatever he wanted, he commanded.

I am giving you wisdom here, wisdom for children, wisdom for marriage, wisdom for lawful status, enough for everything. You will succeed!

Unfortunately for Abigail, she never developed herself mentally, physically, emotionally, or relationally. David was an avid reader;

he was super intelligent and very spiritual. Abigail was wise, but she never took her wisdom to the next level. She did not develop her wisdom to communicate with other queens. Instead, she felt intimidated because she had married a fool.

The foolishness of Nabal rubbed off on Abigail. When Bathsheba showed up, no woman in David's life was able to catch up with her. You may not like her, but she liked herself. She knew how to connect with the prophet. The man who prophesied her doom was the same one who prophesied her glory. Bathsheba developed herself; she became smart and said, *"Hey buddy, this is the king! It was a mistake, but I have taken this mistake and I will overcome it."* She believed in herself. She bowed before the king, but she was so intelligent.

The blessing brings you to a place where the sponsors of sorrow, most times, are those who plot evil. They succeed because you give them room. Develop yourself for the new you that God has risen. Build yourself, learn, grow, be wise, and contribute to dreams. Act everywhere you go; leave your signature, not your stench. Do not let people remember you for being skunky. Let them remember you for your vanilla fragrance. Be that vanilla flower that is both vanilla and lavender. When they come, let them smell your fragrance.

So, at the end of the day, Nabal died for despising David. My prayer for you is that anyone who sponsors sorrow, those foes pretending to be friends will be exposed. Foes do not mean that if you have an interest in something and I have a different interest, I will back off. No! If I have an interest and you have an interest, I will build myself up to the point that your interest becomes invalid.

Backing out does not mean that you do not have an interest. God said, *"Hate him."* You can make someone feel like you love them while actually hating them. I will let you know that I love you, but I have an interest in this, and you have an interest in that. Let the one whose interest is stronger be the possessor of it. That is how God wants it.

The Bible states that the kingdom of God suffers violence, and the violent take it by force. Just make sure that what you are trying to take is what God has authorized you to take. And what is it that God has authorized you to take? It is what He has for you. He told Israel, *"You must not take the land of the Edomites; you must not take the land that I have given to the Ammonites; do not take the land of the sons of Esau or the land of Lot and his children. Any other land, go and take."*

Talkativeness

Proverbs 10:19 (TPT) states: "If you keep talking, it will not be long before you say something really wrong. Prove you are wise from the very start: just bite your tongue and be strong."

When you do not have substance but still talk can lead you to say foolish things. It is just like your body when your kidneys need water. If it cannot find water and you are dehydrated, your kidneys will start looking for anything in your body that is wet to drain, including blood. If your kidneys cannot find anything, they start generating what is called kidney stones because constant dehydration can damage your kidneys.

It is all too easy to fall into the trap of talking without truly saying anything of value. We have all encountered those individuals who seem to have an endless supply of words, yet their conversations leave us feeling empty, drained, or even annoyed. This is of the danger muttering words without substance. You are ultimately leading yourself to a journey of unforeseen consequences and, sorrow. Do not get me wrong. I am not saying you should clam up and never utter a word again. I want you to cultivate an attitude of meaningful conversation, the kind that enriches both the speaker and the listener. If you have got that gift of gab, by all means, use it! But make sure you are not just spewing hot air. Be a man or woman of substance, be someone whose words carry weight and leave a lasting impact.

Think about it for a moment. How many times have you found yourself in a conversation where the other person just will not stop talking, yet you cannot seem to grasp a single meaningful point from whatever they are saying? It is exhausting, is not it? And more often than not, you will find yourself desperately searching for an escape route. Now, imagine being on the other side of that equation. Is that really how you want people to perceive you?

The Bible urges us to *"study to show yourself approved."* This is not hitting the books or memorizing facts. You need to develop a depth of character and understanding that make your words wise in interactions with others. Be able to engage in conversations that go beyond surface-level small talk about things that truly matter.

It said *"let your words be seasoned with grace."* Do not be foolish, do not just sit quietly and say I am being polite because I want season my conversation. You can infuse your speech with kindness, wisdom, and purpose. You can choose your words carefully, and ensure that each one adds value to the conversation and uplifts those around you. The Bible also warns us that *"in the multitude of words, there is bound to be sin."* Now, that is something to chew on, is not it? The more we talk without thinking, the more likely we are to say something we will regret. It is like opening Pandora's box; once those words are out there, you cannot take them back. And before you know it, you might find yourself inadvertently revealing information to people who do not have your best interests at heart.

You see, excessive talkativeness without substance is like a leaky faucet. At first, it might seem harmless, just a bit of dripping here and there. But over time, that constant flow can erode even the sturdiest of foundations. In the same way, mindless chatter can chip away at your credibility, your relationships, and even your self-respect. Let's face it, we live in a world where information is currency. Every word you speak is like a transaction, an exchange of data that can be used for or against you. When you talk without substance, you are essentially giving away valuable intel without getting anything in return. It is like handing out blank checks, you never know who might fill them in and cash them at your expense.

Now, I am not suggesting you become paranoid or start viewing every conversation as a potential threat. But it is crucial to be mindful of what you are saying and to whom. Wise people, the kind of folks you want in your corner, they have got a knack for sniffing out empty talk. And let me tell you, nothing makes them retreat faster than a barrage of meaningless words.

Have you ever found yourself in the middle of a rambling monologue, only to pause and think, *"Wait a minute, am I even making sense right now?"* That moment of self-doubt is your internal alarm system going off, warning you that you have ventured into the dangerous territory of talking without substance. It is your brain's way of saying, *"Hey buddy, maybe it is time to put a sock in it and reassess."* The truth is, substance in conversation is not just about impressing others or avoiding embarrassment. It is about respecting yourself and valuing your own thoughts and ideas enough to present them in a coherent, meaningful way. It is about recognizing that your words have power, the power to inspire, to educate, to comfort, or to harm. And with that power comes the responsibility to use it wisely.

If you find yourself prone to excessive chatter, take a step back and evaluate the content of your conversations. Are you adding value, or are you just filling the air with noise? Are your words building bridges or burning them? Are you leaving people enlightened or exhausted?

If you want to be talkative, be sure you have something worth saying. Otherwise, you might just be paving your own road to sorrow, one meaningless word at a time. Strive to be a person that when you speak, others lean in to listen not because you are loud, but because you are profound.

The Importance Of Meaningful Conversation

Words are not just sounds we utter; they are the building blocks of relationships, the foundation of our society, and the very essence of human connection. When we talk without substance, we are not just wasting breath, we are squandering opportunities to forge genuine connections, to learn, to grow, and to make a real difference in the world around us.

The Bible, gave us a piece of advice: *"Prove from the start that you are wise: do not talk."* Now, at first glance, this might seem contradictory to our discussion about the importance of conversation. But dig a little deeper, and you will find a nugget of pure gold. This is not about maintaining a vow of silence; it is about understanding the power of restraint, of knowing when to speak and when to listen, of recognizing that sometimes, the most profound statements are made in the spaces between words.

Think about the people in your life who you truly respect, the ones whose opinions you value above all others. Chances are, they are not the ones who dominate every conversation with an endless stream of chatter. No, they are likely the ones who speak less but say more, who choose their words carefully and deliver them with precision and impact. That is the kind of wisdom we should all aspire to embody in our conversations. Now, do not get me wrong. I am not advocating for a world of stoic silence. Far from it! There is immense joy to be found in light-hearted banter, in sharing a laugh with a trusted friend, in letting your guard down and just being yourself. These moments of genuine connection are the spice of life, and the strength of any relationships. And let me tell you, there is nothing quite like the comfort of being in the company of someone who truly values you, someone in whose presence you can be your unfiltered self without fear of judgment.

I count myself fortunate to have a handful of such people in my life, friends with whom I can joke, laugh, and engage in playful conversation, knowing full well that they see beyond the surface and appreciate the substance of who I am. These are the relationships that allow us to let our hair down, to explore the lighter side of life without losing sight of myself. It is a delicate balance, but when struck right, it is pure magic.

But not everyone in our lives deserves that level of unfettered access to our thoughts and feelings. We have all encountered those individuals who seem to have a direct line from their ears to the local gossip mill. You share something in confidence, thinking it is just between the two of you, and before you know it, your words are being broadcast far and wide, often distorted beyond recognition. It is experiences like these that teach us the value of discretion, of being selective about what we share and with whom.

You do not say anything in the presence of *"empty-hearted"* people. An empty heart is like a sieve; it cannot hold onto anything of value. When we engage with empty-hearted individuals, our words, no matter how carefully chosen, tend to slip right through, often ending up in places we never intended them to go. You must be vigilant not to become empty-hearted yourself. Because an empty heart leads to an absent mind, and an absent mind leads to careless speech.

You have heard the saying *"think before you leap,"* right? You need to *"think before you speak."* Cultivate that split-second pause before you release them into the air. It is in that pause that wisdom resides, you can choose to elevate your conversations from mindless chatter to meaningful dialogue. It is better to bite your tongue and look strong than to talk endlessly and have others see you as foolish.

Even when you go to the house of God, do not talk too much. The Bible warns us, *"Suffer not your mouth to cause your soul to sin."* How many times have you, in moments of emotional fervor or spiritual ecstasy, made declarations or lofty vows, only to go struggling to live up to them in the cold light of day? We usually say, *"Lord, I give you, my heart; I give you, my soul. I live for you alone,"* in a moment of passion. Then the next day, you find your soul is somewhere else. God says, *"I thought you said you gave me your soul, but you are not living for Me."*

> *Ecclesiastes 5:6: Suffer not thy mouth to cause thy flesh to sin; neither say thou before the angel, that it was an error: wherefore should God be angry at thy voice, and destroy the work of thine hands? We are cautioned not to be hasty in making vows to God, for He takes our promises seriously. You cannot come before God and said I made a mistake.*

So, what is the takeaway from all this? It is simple, engage in meaningful conversations only. Remember, every conversation is an opportunity, an opportunity to learn, to teach, to inspire, to comfort, to challenge, or to be challenged. It is a chance to leave a positive mark on someone's day, to plant a seed of an idea that might grow into something beautiful, or to offer a word of encouragement that could change the trajectory of someone's life.

So, always pause for a moment. Ask yourself: Am I adding value here? Are my words meaningful, or am I just filling the air with noise? Am I honoring the power of speech, or am I squandering it on idle chatter? Let's commit to being people of substance, individuals whose words carry weight and whose conversations leave others feeling enriched, inspired, and valued.

Avoiding Sorrow Through The Control Of Words

You made have heard the saying, *"Sticks and stones may break my bones, but words will never hurt me"*

Well, let me tell you, whoever came up with that clearly never experienced the sting of a well-placed insult or the crushing weight of a carelessly uttered promise. The truth is, words have power, immense power to build up or tear down, to heal or to wound, to bring joy or to invite sorrow. The Bible, in Proverbs 10:19 said:

"In the multitude of words, there is bound to be sin, but he who refrains his tongue is wise."

Now, this is not saying that talking is inherently sinful. No, it is pointing out a fundamental truth about human nature, the more we talk, especially without careful consideration, the more likely we are to say something we should not. It is like playing Russian roulette with our words; the more we pull the trigger, the higher the chances of a misfire.

You see, sorrow does not just ride shotgun with useless talk; it is the inevitable destination of a journey fueled by thoughtless words. Every time we open our mouths without engaging our brains, we are essentially buying a one-way ticket to Regret Ville, population: us. I am not advocating for a vow of silence here. Far from it! Communication is the lifeblood of human interaction, after all. But there is a world of difference between meaningful dialogue and mindless chatter. It is about quality over quantity, substance over noise. If you do not have anything worthwhile to contribute to a conversation, there is no shame in keeping mute. In fact, it might just be the wisest course of action.

> Proverbs 17:28 (NLT): "Even a fool, when he keeps quiet, will be regarded as wise."

It is a bit of divine humor, is not it? The idea that silence can be mistaken for profundity. But there is a deeper truth here, sometimes, the most powerful statement we can make is no statement at all. It is about having the discernment to know when to speak and when to listen, when to contribute and when to contemplate. But let's be clear, this is not a blanket endorsement of silence in all situations. There are times when speaking up is not just important, it is crucial. If you are in a meeting and you have valuable insights to share, do not let fear of rejection or past experiences of being overlooked hold you back. That is not wisdom; that is the spirit of slavery working overtime to keep you small and silent. You have a voice, and it deserves to be heard.

The Bible tells said, *"Where the words of a king are, there is power."* You might not wear a crown, but in your sphere of influence, be it your workplace, your community, or your family, your words carry weight. When you choose not to speak up in situations where your input is needed, you are essentially abdicating your power, leaving a vacuum that others may fill with less worthy contributions. If you have been part of a team where your previous opinions were disregarded, do not let that experience silence you permanently. Instead, use it as motivation to work on yourself, to refine your ideas, and to develop more effective ways of communicating. Then, armed with newfound confidence and clarity, speak up again. Your perspective matters, and the world needs to hear it.

Some men have mouths suffering from diarrhea. Yes, verbal diarrhea. These are people who cannot seem to stop talking, who believe that the sheer volume of their words somehow equates to the rightness of their opinions. It is as if their mouths are engaged in a marathon while their brains are taking a leisurely stroll in the park. These are the *"harvesters of sorrow"* we mentioned earlier. They sow words indiscriminately and reap a crop of misunderstandings, hurt feelings, and damaged relationships.

If you find yourself falling into this category (and let's, be honest, we all do at times), it is time for some serious self-reflection. Ask yourself: Am I talking because I have something valuable to contribute, or am I just filling the silence? Am I speaking from a place of knowledge and understanding, or am I just repeating half-baked ideas and unverified information? Remember, it is not about having an opinion on everything; it is about having well-informed, thoughtful perspectives on the things that truly matter.

You need to be a man or woman of substance. Develop your character, expand your knowledge base, and hon your critical thinking skills. Be able to engage in meaningful dialogue on a wide range of topics, not just superficial small talk. When you speak from a place of substance, your words carry weight. They inspire, they challenge, they enlighten.

Sorrow Corrupts Your Heart With Wickedness

Proverbs 10:20 (TPT): "The teachings of the godly ones are like pure silver, bringing words of redemption to others. But the heart of the wicked is corrupted with sorrow, making them reject pure, destiny-molding teachings."

Chew this spiritual meat first. This is not some flowery words strung together to sound pretty. No, sir! It is a this is a divine warning, a divine heads-up if you will, about the insidious nature of sorrow and its power to twist our hearts, turning us away from the very teachings that could shape our destinies for the better. You see, sorrow are not just about feeling down in the dumps or having a bad day. I am showing you a deep-seated, soul-crushing kind of sorrow that takes root in the hearts and starts growing like a weed, choking out the good stuff. It is the kind of sorrow that makes us cynical, bitter, and resistant to anything that might actually help us get out of our miserable state. It is like we are wearing sorrow-tinted glasses, and suddenly everything looks bleak and hopeless.

But this sorrow-induced wickedness does not just affect you alone. It is got a ripple effect that touches everyone around. While the godly are out there dropping pearls of wisdom like pure silver, bringing redemption and hope to those who'll listen, the sorrow-corrupted heart is busy rejecting these life-changing teachings. It is like turning away from a feast because you have convinced yourself that you are destined to starve. Nobody is perfect. We all make mistakes, and that is just part of being human. The real tragedy is not in making mistakes; it is in refusing to correct them. It is in living and dying with those mistakes, stubbornly rejecting the very teachings that could set you free. It is like being lost in a dark forest and refusing to follow the trail of breadcrumbs that could lead you back home.

So, what is a person to do in the face of this sorrow-induced wickedness? Well, I will tell you what, you have to make up your mind, right here and now, to be hungry for the pure truth. And I am not talking about a little snack-sized hunger. I am talking about a ravenous, all-consuming appetite for truth that will not be satisfied with anything less than the real deal. This is not going to be a walk in the park, mind you. Truth, real truth, is demanding. It is challenging. It will push you out of your comfort zone and make you question everything you thought you knew. But that is exactly what we should be excited about! When truth challenges us, it is not trying to break us down; it is building us up, shaping us into the people we are meant to be.

It is not just about saying the truth, either. That is the easy part. No, the real game-changer is knowing the truth. It is about letting that truth seep into every fiber of your being, transforming you from the inside out. It is about living the truth, breathing the truth, becoming the truth.

Now, every time you find yourself stumbling around in the dark, feeling lost and confused, there is one question you need to ask yourself: *"What do I need to know that I do not know?"* Most times, the things we do not know are not really unknown at all. They are the very things God is been trying to tell us all along, but our hearts have been too clouded, too darkened by sorrow and wickedness to let that light shine through. The Bible tells us that if our hearts are clouded, the light of truth cannot penetrate. And if that light cannot get through, we are just going to keep on walking down that path of error, stumbling and falling and wondering why we cannot seem to get it right. It is like trying to read a map in the dark, you might think you are heading in the right direction, but you are really just going in circles.

And let me tell you, error is no joke. It is the chief sponsor of sorrow, the big boss behind all our heartache and pain. You see, mistakes are just wrong moves, like taking a wrong turn on a road trip. But if you do not address those mistakes, if you do not pull over and check the map, those wrong turns become full-blown errors. And errors, my friends, they bring with them the spirit of slavery.

I am not talking about physical chains here. I am talking about a spiritual bondage that is just as real and just as devastating. It is the kind of bondage that has kings and princes walking on foot while servants and slaves ride on horses. It is a complete reversal of the natural order, a topsy-turvy world where everything is out of whack. And some of you out there are suffering from this very thing right now. You are experiencing the sorrow of error, walking barefoot on the rocky path of life when you should be riding high on your horse of destiny. You are struggling and striving when you should be thriving, all because you have let sorrow corrupt your heart and turn you away from the very teachings that could set you free.

But here is the good news, it does not have to stay this way. You do not have to remain a slave to sorrow and error. You have the power to change your situation, to break free from the chains of wickedness and step into the light of truth. It starts with recognizing the problem, with understanding that sorrow has been corrupting your heart and clouding your judgment.

The next step is to make that decision to talked about earlier, the decision to be hungry for truth, no matter how challenging or uncomfortable it might be. It is about opening your heart and your mind to the teachings that can shape your destiny, even if they go against everything you thought you knew. Every mistake is an opportunity for growth, every error a chance for correction. But you have to be willing to face those mistakes head-on, to admit when you are wrong and be open to change. It is not easy, but I promise you, it is worth it.

You see, at the end of the day, we all have a choice. You can let sorrow corrupt your heart and lead you down a path of wickedness and error, or you can embrace the truth, no matter how demanding it may be, and allow it to shape your destinies for the better. The choice is yours. What will you choose?

CHAPTER NINE

KEYS OF THE BLESSING THAT ANNIHILATE SORROW AND SUFFERING

◆ ◆ ◆

TRUST GOD

◆ ◆ ◆

Jeremiah 17:7-8 (LBT): "Blessed is the man who trusts in the Lord."

When you truly trust in the Lord, it does not matter what kind of heat comes your way. Life can throw its worst at us, but you will be standing tall like a tree planted by the riverside, unmoved and unshaken. Why? Because your roots run deep into the soil of God is faithfulness.

Trusting God is not just about saying, *"Oh, I believe in God"* and then living your life like He does not exist. No, no, no! You have to cultivate a deep, unshakeable confidence in His character, His promises, and His unwavering love for you. You have wake up every morning and declaring, *"God, I do not know what today holds, but I know who holds today, and that is enough for me."*

You have got to understand, friends, that trust is the currency of the Kingdom. It is what moves the hand of God in your favor. When you trust God, you are essentially saying, *"Lord, I surrender my limited understanding, my finite wisdom, and my puny strength to Your infinite knowledge, Your boundless wisdom, and Your almighty power."* And let me tell you, when you make that exchange, you are setting yourself up for a life of supernatural interventions and divine orchestrations.

But trust is not built overnight. It is not some microwave miracle that pops up at the press of a button. No, it is cultivated through consistent fellowship with God, through studying His Word, through experiencing His faithfulness in the small things. It is built through those quiet moments when you are alone with God, pouring out your heart to Him, and allowing His presence to permeate every fiber of your being. You have got to understand that trusting God is a choice you make every single day. It is a decision to believe that God is who He says He is, that He will do what He says He will do, even when your circumstances are screaming the opposite. It is choosing to stand on God is promises when everything around you are crumbling. It is declaring, *"Though He slay me, yet will I trust Him,"* like Job did in the midst of his suffering.

Now, let me tell you something, friends. When you make that choice to trust God, come rain or shine, you are positioning yourself for a life of unparalleled blessings. You are setting yourself up for a life where sorrow and suffering do not have the final say. Why? Because when you trust God, you are tapping into a source of joy, peace, and strength that transcends your circumstances. Think about it, when you trust God, you are not easily shaken by the storms of life. You do not lose sleep over every little problem because you know you serve a God who neither slumbers nor sleeps. You do not get worked up over every negative report because you know that your God is able to turn every curse into a blessing. That is the power of trust!

But let me warn you, this trust I am talking about is not some passive, wishy-washy sentiment. No, it is an active, dynamic force that propels you into bold action. When you trust God, you step out in faith even when you cannot see the entire staircase. You launch out into the deep even when the waters look turbulent. Why? Because you know that the God who called you is faithful, and He will do it! Trusting God does not mean you will not face challenges. It does not mean life will always be a bed of roses. No, but it means that in the midst of those challenges, in the heat of those trials, you have an anchor for your soul. You have a rock on which you stand, unmoved and unshaken.

You see, when you trust God, you develop what I call a *"nevertheless"* mentality. The doctor's report may be negative, nevertheless, you trust in the God who is your healer. Your bank account may be in the red, nevertheless, you trust in the God who is your provider. Your relationships may be in shambles, nevertheless, you trust in the God who is the restorer of the breach. That is the power of trust!

You have got to understand that when you trust God, you are not just hoping for the best; you are expecting the best because you know who your God is. You are not walking around with your head hanging low, defeated and dejected. No! You are walking with your head held high, your shoulders squared, because you know that greater is He that is in you than he that is in the world. Trust activates the supernatural in your life. It opens up channels of divine intervention that you never knew existed. When you trust God, you are essentially giving Him permission to move in your life in extraordinary ways. You are saying, *"God, I may not understand it all, but I trust You to work it all out for my good."*

How deep is your trust in God? Is it surface level, or does it run deep into the core of your being? Is your trust in God strong enough to withstand the storms of life, or does it crumble at the first sign of trouble? These are questions you need to honestly answer because the depth of your trust will determine the height of your blessing. Shallow trust produces shallow results. But deep, unwavering trust? Oh, that is what moves mountains! That is what parts Red Seas! That is what brings down walls of Jericho! That is what turns water into wine! That is the kind of trust that annihilates sorrow and suffering from your life completely.

When you truly trust in the Lord, you become unstoppable. Why? Because you are no longer limited by your own abilities or constrained by your circumstances. You are now operating in the realm of the limitless God! The God who says, *"Is anything too hard for me?"* The God who declares, *"Behold, I am the Lord, the God of all flesh. Is there anything too hard for me?"* I challenge you today, deepen your trust in God. Make it your life's mission to know Him more intimately, to trust Him more completely. Spend time in His presence. Meditate on His word day and night. Reflect on His faithfulness in your past. As you do this, you will find your trust growing stronger, becoming an unshakeable foundation for your life.

Blessed is the man who trusts in the Lord. Not the man who trusts in his own strength. Not the man who trusts in his bank account. Not the man who trusts in his connections. No, blessed is the man who puts his trust fully and completely in the Lord. That man, that woman, will be like a tree planted by the waters, flourishing even in times of drought, bearing fruit in every season. I want you to make a decision right now. Decide that from this moment on, your trust will be firmly anchored in God. Decide that no matter what comes your way, your first response will be to trust God. Decide that you will no longer be moved by what you see, but you will be anchored by what God has said.

Trust in the Lord with all your heart, and lean not on your own understanding. In all your ways acknowledge Him, and He shall direct your paths. That is a life of victory, a life where sorrow and suffering do not have the last word.

Obedience

Isaiah 1:19: "If you are willing and obedient, you shall eat the good of the land."

Oh, glory to God! Can you see the promise packed into that single verse? It said you shall eat; now eating here is not about food, it was a metaphor that described the experience of having the fullness of God is blessings in every area of your life.

You see, obedience does not just mean that you are following a set of dos and don'ts. It brings your a plan where you heart align with the plan, purpose and will of God. It brings you to place of absolute surrender to His perfect plan. That is when you can say like Jesus, *"God, not my will, but Your will be done."* And let me tell you, when you make that decision to obey God, come hell or high water, you are setting yourself up for a life of abundance that will blow your mind!

Understand this: Obedience is not a suggestion in the Kingdom of God. It is not an option that you can take or leave. No, it is a command, a divine imperative that opens the floodgates of Heaven's blessings into your life. When God says, *"If you obey and serve Him, you will spend your days in prosperity and your years in plenty,"* He is not making a casual observation. He is giving us a spiritual blueprint for success! This is more than just doing what God says when it is convenient or when it aligns with your own desires. True obedience is doing what God says even when it does not make sense to your natural mind. It is obeying God even when every fiber of your being is screaming, *"This is crazy!"* That is when your obedience really counts.

Again, remember When God told Abraham in Genesis 6 to leave his father's house and go to a land He would show him. Now, in those days, leaving your father's house was like committing social suicide. It meant leaving behind your inheritance, your social standing, everything! But Abraham obeyed. He packed up and left, not even knowing where he was going. And what was the result? God blessed him so much that he became the father of many nations. We saw that already.

God told Noah to build an ark when there was not a cloud in the sky. Can you imagine the ridicule he faced? People probably thought he had lost his mind. But Noah obeyed, and his obedience saved not just his family, but the entire human race! That is the power of obedience! Let me tell you, obedience positions you for blessing. It aligns you with God is perfect will for your life. When you obey God, you are essentially saying, *"God, I trust Your plan more than my own. I believe Your wisdom is higher than my understanding."* And let me tell you, when you take that posture of obedience, God moves Heaven and Earth to bless you!

Obedience requires sacrifice. It will say go against the grain, swimming upstream when everyone else is floating downstream. It will cost you to give up on relationship that God has told you to let go of. It also goes with forgiving that person who hurt you deeply. It stretches you. It challenges you. But let me tell you, it is in that place of obedience, in that place of surrender, that God does His greatest work in your life. It is in that place of obedience that miracles happen, that breakthroughs come, that destinies are fulfilled!

When you cultivate that lifestyle of obedience, you begin to experience what the Bible calls *"the good of the land."* Your days become filled with prosperity not just financial prosperity, but prosperity in every area of your life. Your relationships prosper. Your health prospers. Your mind prospers; your ministry prospers. Everything you put your hand to begins to prosper!

But do not get it twisted. This prosperity I am talking about is not just about having a fat bank account or driving the latest car. Although it is applicable, but am taking that experience that comes with enjoying the fullness of God is blessings in every area of your life. It covers your health. It gives you peace that passes all understanding. It gives you joy unspeakable and full of glory. That is what happens when you obey God! It activates God is promises in your life. You see, God promises are not automatic. They are not like some vending machine where you insert your coin and out pops your blessing. No, God promises are activated by your obedience. When you obey God, you are essentially pulling down Heaven's blessings into your earthly reality.

Now, how is your obedience quotient? Are you quick to obey God, or do you drag your feet? Do you obey God fully, or do you pick and choose which parts of His Word you want to follow? These are critical questions because the level of your obedience will determine the level of your blessing. You see, partial obedience is still disobedience. When God tells you to do something, He is not looking for you to meet Him halfway. He is not interested in compromise. He wants total, complete, unreserved obedience. That is what moves His hand in your favor. That is what releases the fullness of His blessings into your life.

When you obey God, you are not doing God a favor. You are not adding anything to His greatness or His glory. No, you are positioning yourself to receive what He has already prepared for you. You are aligning yourself with His perfect will, which is always for your good. Prophet Samuel said "…..*To obey is better than sacrifice. (1 kings 15:22)*" You can offer God all the sacrifices in the world, but if you are not walking in obedience, those sacrifices mean nothing. God is more interested in your obedience than in your religious activities. He is more concerned about your heart's alignment with His will than with your outward show of piety.

I want you to make a decision right now. Decide that from this moment on, you will be quick to obey God. Decide that no matter what He asks of you, your answer will be a resounding *"Yes, Lord!"* Decide that you will no longer let fear, doubt, or human reasoning hold you back from walking in complete obedience to God. Obey God, and watch how He turns your life around. Watch how He annihilates sorrow and suffering from your life. Watch how He opens doors that no man can shut. Watch how He makes a way where there seems to be no way. Watch how He takes you from the background and puts you in the forefront. Watch how He lifts you from the miry clay and sets your feet upon a rock.

Love The Lord

I have shown you the place of trust and obedience and what they contribute to annihilate sorrow from your life. But those two together have a language that summarize their operations in our lives. Paul said in 1 Corinthians 2:9:

> *"Eyes have not seen, ears have not heard, neither has it entered into the heart of man the things God has prepared for them that love Him."*

There is indeed a blessing that God as prepared for you and I that Paul want us to see as the result of our love for him.

You see, this not that emotional things you know. It is not just that saying, *"Oh, I love You, Lord"* when everything is going well. No, it goes down to having a deep, unshakeable commitment to God that stands firm even when the storms of life are raging. It brings out a passion for God that consumes everything that want to distract you and influences every decision you make, that shapes your entire worldview.

The Bible says that God commands and enjoys blessings beyond human understanding for those who love Him. That means when you make loving God your priority, you are setting yourself up for a life of supernatural favor, divine orchestrations, and miraculous interventions. You are positioning yourself to experience blessings that will make your head spin! Jesus said,

"If you love Me, keep My commandments." Our love for God is demonstrated through your obedience, through your willingness to align your life with His Word. When you love God, His desires become your desires. His priorities become your priorities. His heartbeat becomes your heartbeat.

The Bible calls David a man after God is own heart. Why? Because David loved God with a passion that was unmatched. Even when he messed up, even when he fell into sin, his love for God always brought him back to a place of repentance and restoration. And what was the result? God blessed David beyond measure, established his throne forever, and even promised that the Messiah would come from his lineage! When you love the Lord, you command and enjoy blessings beyond human understanding. Your love for God becomes a magnet that attracts divine favor into every area of your life. When you love God, you are no longer operating in the realm of the ordinary. You are stepping into a dimension of the supernatural where miracles become your daily bread!

Love works hand and hand with sacrifice. It will always putt God is will above your own desires. It will always give up on relationship that is pulling you away from God. It will always forgive people who hurt you deeply. It will always step out in faith to pursue it God-given vision, even when it does not make sense to your natural mind. The lord of God will take you out of your comfort zone. It challenges you. It stretches you. This is what it means to say *"things which eye has not seen and ear has not heard."* Your life becomes a testimony of God is goodness. People look at you and wonder, "How is this person so blessed? How do they have so much peace in the midst of chaos? How do they remain joyful even in difficult circumstances?" And the answer is simple, it is because you love God!

The blessings that come from loving God are not just material blessings. Yes, God can and will bless you materially, but that is just the tip of the iceberg. When you love God, you experience a peace that passes all understanding. You walk in a joy that is not dependent on circumstances. You have a confidence that comes from knowing you are loved by the father. That is the real blessing of loving God!

Love activates His promises in your life. God promises are not just nice sayings to make you feel good. They are rock-solid guarantees backed by the integrity of God Himself. And when you love God, you position yourself to experience the fullness of those promises in your life. You become a partner with God in bringing His will to pass in your life and in the world around you. You become a vessel of His love, a channel of His power, a demonstration of His glory. And in that place of loving God, sorrow and suffering lose their grip on your life.

So, make loving God your top priority. Do not just love God when it is convenient or when things are going well. Love Him even when it is difficult. Love Him even when you do not understand what He is doing. Love Him even when everyone around you is turning away from Him. Because it is in that place of unwavering love for God that He shows up and shows out in your life! Jesus said the greatest commandment is to love the Lord your God with all your heart, soul, mind, and strength. This is not just a suggestion; it is a command. And when you obey this command, when you make loving God your life's mission, you position yourself for blessings that will blow your mind!

Love God, and watch how He transforms your life. Watch how He annihilates sorrow and suffering from your existence. Watch how He opens doors of opportunity that you never even knew existed. Watch how He makes a way where there seems to be no way. Watch how He takes you from the pit and puts you on the mountaintop. Watch how He turns your mourning into dancing and your sorrow into joy. Loving the Lord is your key to a life of supernatural blessings. It is your ticket to experiencing things that eye has not seen, ear has not heard, and that have not even entered into the heart of man to imagine.

The Prophetic Declaration Of God Is Prophet Or Your Spiritual Covering

The prophet of God assigned over your life annihilates sorrow and enforces blessing. When they were struggling to build, they were struggling until Zechariah came and began to prophesy. They prospered through the prophecy of the servants of God. Every time God wants to let a person know that He loves and cares for them, He provides a spiritual covering.

The Bible says there was a time in Israel when they were without a teaching priest (2 Chronicles 15). Without a true prophet, everyone did whatever they wanted to do without guidance. As a result, God allowed all manner of adversities to come upon them. Things kept going wrong until the prophet of God came and said to the king, *"Take courage and do the right thing in the eyes of God."* When the prophet gave them instruction, they started seeking God, reversed their circumstances, and God gave them rest.

> *"But ye men of Judah gave up the good work, and do not get discouraged, for you will be rewarded."*

When the prophet tells you that this day God will bless you, believe it. In verse 8, *"the prophet told the king, 'I had this message from God: Take courage.'"*

The voice of your prophet gives you courage, but courage that is given requires that you take action. Courage will not take you; you have to take it. He took courage and destroyed all the altars, the sources of sorrow, the evil idols. When he destroyed them, what happened? Suddenly, they decided to serve God. The Bible tells us in verse 15 that they all served God, vowed, and sought Him with one heart. When they made that vow to serve the Lord, God gave them rest on every side.

All were happy for this covenant with God because they had

entered into it with all their hearts and wills, wanting Him above everything else. They found Him, and He gave them peace throughout the nation.

When God wanted to punish Israel, the Bible says He took away their prophets. For 400 years, no one could hear from the Lord. When one man appeared, he started his ministry in the wilderness, and all the people left the town. They had their Jewish religious leaders, but they knew they were quoting scriptures without having the word of the Lord. When John the Baptist showed up in the wilderness, they recognized he was from God, so they went searching for him. Despite John calling them names, they did not care; they said, *"Call us whatever names you want; we need God."*

Saul insulted the prophet God had given him. One day, when he needed to hear from God, he boycotted his prophet, thinking, *"Forget that; I will get the priest."* The same demon that wanted to destroy his prophet led him to destroy the priests. So he went to the priest, but the Bible says God would not speak to Saul not through Urim, not through dreams, nor through a prophet. All avenues of God is voice were shut off from his life.

> *"And Saul inquired of the Lord, and the Lord answered him not, neither by dreams, nor by Urim, nor by prophets."*

He was left in the dark. When God wants to punish a person, He keeps that person in the dark. He will not give them a prophet over their life.

So, when you say, *"I do not believe in any prophet; I do not believe in a man of God over my life; I do not want anybody to control me,"* It is a clear sign that God has given them over to a reprobate mind. True prophets of God are not seeking to control you; they are agents of intervention called by God to bring blessings into your life. Prophets are carriers of blessings, genuine ones. When they show up in your life, sorrows are arrested; sorrows are eliminated.

Even Bathsheba's sorrow was transformed into joy by the prophet Nathan. If Bathsheba's sorrow can be changed into joy, what cannot God do by blessing you through me? God sent me to you, and I am not ashamed of that. Paul said, *"I magnify my office."* So together, we will take over this nation.

Do not despise your prophets; otherwise, God will stop communicating with you. God wants to talk to you directly, but often, people are too busy or too distracted to hear. There are people He has called to speak on His behalf so that those who are not hearing and those who hear well can communicate effectively.

They asked Jesus, *"What can we do to do the works of God?"* He said, *"The works of God are simple: believe in Him whom He sent."* Jesus told His disciples, *"As the Father has sent Me, so I send you."* God sent me to wipe away your tears and bring you into the fullness of what God has for your life by unlocking His blessings.

> The Bible says in Ezekiel 34:26: *"I will cause to come down showers in His season, and there shall be showers of blessings."*

You must learn to challenge God is blessings in your life; otherwise, you will never maximize the blessings of God.

the essence intact: It is very possible to have the best life if you master the art of referring your life's challenges to the blessings of God upon your life or upon your lineage. Blessings are spiritual specialists that release the power, aroma, and fortune needed to give you the life you desire or the life God has promised you.

When you master certain spiritual principles, you will begin to rule. If you do not show excitement over your redemption, it will be withdrawn from you. Excitement validates the license of believers. When your greatest pride is in the life you used to have or in the blessings you once possessed, that is the spirit of the tail. Every month ought to be a harvest season. When you find yourself being attacked by the spirit of the tail, you must refer the spirit of the tail to the blessing of the head.

When you refer your battles to the right specialist, knowing the right things to do and taking your position, over time, your life will begin to work again. What Satan hates the most is for you to catch the secret and unction of being anointed. You must fight for the blessing. You must decide to be blessed and make sense of your life.

If you do not know how to regrow lost hair, your family altar will be the most useless altar. *(Judges 16:22)*. When God says, *"I will bless you and make your name great, and you will be a blessing,"* He means He is establishing something within you that will continually flow so that others can take from it.

When God places a blessing on you, good things grow. Personalize this: declare,

> *"The blessings on my life will cause good things to grow wherever I go."*

Do not be afraid, make that next move! Whatever you will ever need is available.

CHAPTER TEN

THE PURPOSE OF
THE BLESSING

The purpose of the blessing is twofold, and you better grab hold of this truth with both hands. It is either bringing you closer to it or bringing it closer to you. It is like a spiritual magnet, constantly at work in your life, aligning you with God is divine plan and purpose. When God blesses you, He is not just handing you a gift and walking away. No, He is setting in motion a divine orchestration that is designed to draw you deeper into His presence, deeper into His will, deeper into the fullness of all He has for you. It is like He is saying, "Come closer, my child. There is more where that came from!"

But it does not stop there. It gets even better! Sometimes, when you cannot seem to move any closer to the blessing, God, in His infinite mercy and love, brings the blessing closer to you. He is not just sitting on some far-off throne, uninterested in our daily struggles. No, He is an ever-present help in time of need, ready to move Heaven and Earth to position you for blessing!

> *1 Kings 17:15-16: And she went and did according to the saying of Elijah: and she, and he, and her house, did eat many days. And the barrel of meal wasted not, neither did the cruse of oil fail, according to the word of the LORD, which he spake by Elijah.*

The widow of Zarephath, who was down to her last meal, experienced a miracle that defied natural laws. The flour in the bin did not run out, and the oil in the jar did not run dry. Why? Because the Word of God had spoken it into existence! You have got to understand that when God speaks a blessing over your life, it is not just empty words. It is a creative force that brings into existence things that do not exist. It is a sustaining power that keeps you going even when all-natural resources have been exhausted. That is the power of the blessing!

God, the commander of the blessing, knows exactly what's contained within that blessing. He is not shooting in the dark, hoping something good will happen to you. No, He is purposeful, intentional, and strategic in His blessings. He knows the end from the beginning, and He is packed into your blessing everything you need for life and godliness.

But walking in the blessing does not mean you will not face challenges. It does not mean everyone will suddenly start throwing rose petals at your feet. No, you will still encounter people who, in their foolishness, will try to provoke you, to pull you down to their level. But here is where the rubber meets the road, when they show their foolishness, you respond with wisdom. When they display their stupidity, you respond with dignity.

One of the most beautiful aspects of choosing the blessing, it comes with a peace pack. Oh, hallelujah! This is not just any kind of peace. This is the peace that passes all understanding. It is a peace that guards your heart and mind in Christ Jesus. It is a peace that travels with you throughout your life, no matter what storms may rage around you. And let me tell you, this peace is a double-edged sword. On one side, it keeps you calm and collected in the face of adversity. On the other side, it confounds your enemies, who cannot understand how you can remain so composed when everything seems to be falling apart. That is the power of the peace that comes with the blessing!

Now, the thereabouts four aspects of the blessings.

First, we have the power of the blessing. the raw, unadulterated power from on high. It is the same power that raised Christ from the dead, and guess what? It is at work in you right now! Then we have the place of the blessing. He blesses you for a purpose, and that purpose is often tied to a specific place, your place of assignment. When you are walking in obedience, operating in your God-given purpose, that is when you experience the fullness of the blessing.

Then the flow of the blessing. When God opens the windows of heaven, it is not just a trickle of blessing. It is a flood! It is an overwhelming, overflowing abundance that not only meets your needs but positions you to be a blessing to others. The blessing of God in your life should be so evident that it splashes onto everyone around you! And the force from the blessing. This is the momentum, the spiritual energy that propels you forward even when circumstances try to hold you back. It is what keeps you moving, keeps you believing, keeps you achieving even when the odds are stacked against you.

> Ezekiel 34:26 says, "I will cause showers to come down in their season; they will be showers of blessing."

When God sends these showers, He will cause you to be blessed. Not might, not could, but will! It is a divine guarantee, backed by the integrity of God Himself!

The blessing of God in your life is not just for your comfort or convenience. It is a divine strategy to position you for greatness, to align you with God is purpose, and to make you a channel of His goodness to the world around you. When you walk in the blessing, you become a living, breathing testament to His goodness. Your life becomes a billboard advertising the faithfulness of God. People look at you and see not just your success, but the hand of God at work in your life.

CONCLUSION

What a time it is with my friends, it becomes clear that the blessing is far more than just a promise of prosperity or success, it is the very force that God has designed to expel sorrow from our lives. The spiritual principles revealed in these pages are not simply for reflection, but for action. They are meant to realign our lives with God is will, ensuring that we not only receive His blessings but also live in a way that those blessings annihilate every trace of sorrow.

From the beginning, we understood that planting bitter seeds will always bring a bitter harvest. You cannot expect good fruit from a corrupted seed, and many people spend their lives sowing bitterness while hoping for joy. God is law of sowing and reaping is unchangeable, and it is a reminder that we need to be conscious of the seeds we plant each day. If we expect blessings, then we must ensure that the seeds we plant are rooted in faith, kindness, and obedience to God. Only by changing what we sow can we expect to receive the harvest that God desires for us.

The promises of God come with great responsibilities, and they require more from us than just sitting and waiting. We explored how Abraham received a promise from God but had to endure years of waiting before seeing the fulfillment. During that time, he was tempted to take matters into his own hands, and many of us are guilty of the same. But God promises are not meant to be fulfilled through shortcuts, they demand obedience, patience, and trust in His perfect timing. When we align ourselves with these principles, we not only wait for God promises but we prepare ourselves for the weight of the blessing that is coming.

Mining the blessing is not a passive endeavor. We learned that blessings are like treasures hidden beneath the surface, waiting to be uncovered by those who are willing to dig deep. This requires effort and perseverance. Too often, people receive a word of blessing and expect it to unfold without any effort on their part. But God blessings must be worked, engaged with, and cultivated. It is through this process of working the blessing that we develop the character and spiritual depth necessary to fully experience the richness of God is favor.

The type of blessing we pursue is also crucial. Not every blessing has the power to drive out sorrow completely. There is a special kind of blessing that overflows, that does not just cover sorrow but flushes it out entirely. This blessing goes beyond material wealth or temporary victories, it is the deep, soul-satisfying favor of God that touches every area of our lives. When we set our hearts on this kind of blessing, we align ourselves with God is eternal purposes, and sorrow has no place to take root.

But this kind of blessing does not come without a fight. Just as Jacob wrestled with God for his blessing, we are called to contend for ours. We must not be passive observers in our spiritual walk, hoping that God will simply hand us what we desire. Sorrow will always try to attach itself to our blessings, but we have the authority to fight back. The enemy understands the value of the blessing and will do everything in his power to prevent us from walking in it. But when we stand firm in faith, persistent in prayer, and determined in our pursuit of God's promises, we will see the blessing come to pass without sorrow.

The assignment of the blessing is another essential truth we cannot ignore. God does not bless us just for our own comfort or satisfaction. Every blessing carries a purpose beyond us. When God blesses us, He is looking to use that blessing to impact others, to fulfill His greater plan on the earth. Abraham's blessing was not just for him; it was meant to bless nations. In the same way, the blessings we receive are meant to extend beyond our personal lives. When we understand this, we shift from selfish ambition to being vessels through which God's goodness can flow to the world.

One of the most difficult lessons we have had to learn is about God's timing. There are times when doors we are praying for remain closed, not because God has forgotten about us, but because He is preparing something greater. These delays are not denials; they are divine strategies. During these waiting periods, God is aligning everything according to His will, preparing us for a blessing that exceeds our expectations. When we trust in His timing, we realize that the waiting is not wasted, it is a critical part of the process that prepares us to handle the fullness of what God wants to give us.

Sorrow comes in many forms, and it often disguises itself in garments we do not expect. It can show up in disappointment, in loss, in unmet expectations. But the blessing of God gives us the power to cast off these garments of sorrow. We are not meant to walk in heaviness, constantly burdened by the challenges of life. Even when sorrow tries to attach itself to our lives, God has given us the tools to overcome it through faith, prayer, and the power of His blessing. The garments of sorrow will be replaced with the robe of praise when we learn to trust fully in the sufficiency of God's grace.

Intelligence prayer plays a key role in eradicating sorrow from our lives. We saw how Jabez prayed specifically and boldly, asking God not just to bless him, but to keep sorrow far from him. This is the kind of prayer we must learn to pray intentional, direct, and full of faith. When we approach God with this level of clarity and trust, we open the door for Him to move powerfully in our lives. The blessing that eliminates sorrow is not something that happens by chance; it is the result of engaging with God intentionally and aligning our hearts with His will.

the purpose of every blessing is to establish God is covenant on the earth. We are blessed to be a blessing. The favor that God bestows upon us is not meant to end with us but to flow through us to others. Our lives, when fully surrendered to God, become conduits of His goodness, His mercy, and His provision. The blessings call us to bring others into the same experience, using what we have been given to advance His kingdom and glorify His name.

ABOUT THE BOOK

The Blessing - The Eradicator of Sorrow is a revelation of God's divine plan to lift His children out of the cycle of sorrow. This is not just another book, it is a spiritual manual designed to unveil the mystery of the blessing, showing how it is the key to silencing sorrow and unlocking a life filled with God is abundance. The blessing God gives is not tied to material wealth or temporary victories, but to a deeper, supernatural grace that transforms lives from within.

This book reveals the force to contended with for the blessings to be manifested, the treasure that must be mined with faith, purpose, and perseverance. When God is blessing rests upon you, it does not just cover up sorrow, it drives it out completely, leaving no trace behind. Sorrow may come in many forms, but the blessing of God is powerful enough to flush out every root of pain and loss that seeks to attach itself to your life.

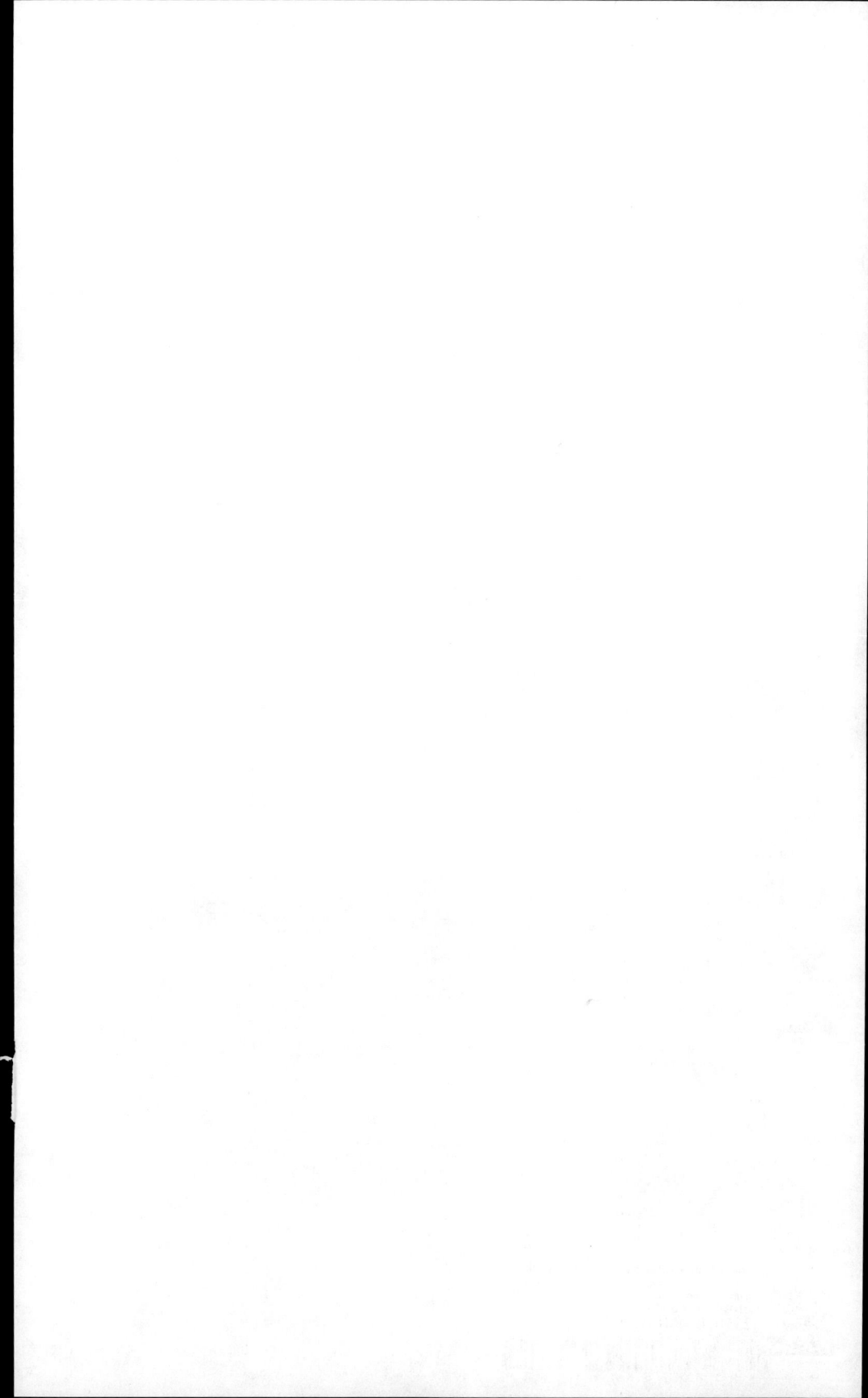

www.ingramcontent.com/pod-product-compliance
Lightning Source LLC
Chambersburg PA
CBHW071858020426
42331CB00010B/2567